Praise for Michael E. Gerber, Peter Weinstein, DVM, MBA, and *The E-Myth Veterinarian*

I read this book in just two days while on a trip because I didn't want to put it down! How wonderful to read a book with concepts from such an esteemed author as Michael Gerber, but then to have the content applied specifically to veterinary medicine by such a respected veterinary thought leader, Peter Weinstein. As I read the book, I thought of how many of my clients could benefit from the book's insights. The authors' unique perspective on managing systems instead of people, and real-world examples provides you with an action plan to grow your practice and have a successful business. Weinstein is candid, entertaining, and enlightening. **I highly recommend you read this book if you are a practice owner or in any way involved in helping veterinary practice leaders.** It will inspire you to make changes to have the career and life you want and deserve.

Amanda L. Donnelly, DVM, MBA, President and Owner,
ALD Veterinary Consulting, LLC

Peter's wide breadth of experience in our profession has certainly paid dividends in the writing of this book. As an associate, owner, consultant, and leader in organized veterinary medicine, he brings a point of view that is unique. *The E-Myth Veterinarian* is a wonderful book—congratulations are in order for both Peter and Michael.

Tom Carpenter, DVM, Newport Harbor Animal Hospital

Work IN your practice or work ON your practice? **This book is not only a thump between the eyes on why to change, it is also a guide on how to make the change.** Dr. Weinstein's insight and experience drive home the E-Myth concepts and their application to your veterinary practice. This should be mandatory reading for all current and future practice owners.

David McCormick, MS, CVA, Simmons and Associates

The E-Myth Veterinarian says it all. It approaches all five phases of a business in great detail. Peter Weinstein, DVM, is uniquely knowledgeable, cares about the veterinary industry, is extremely proactive, and has a handle on all the issues in the industry, as well as the day-to-day challenges that all practice owners experaience. Peter has a dream for himself and the veterinary industry—he wants the veterinary industry to improve, and he will go to extreme lengths (like writing a book) to make that happen. **The content, clarity, and organization of this book will captivate you and make you a better person and veterinarian.**

Louis M. Gatto, CPA, Gatto McFerson,
www.gattomcferson.com

Peter Weinstein is a long-time friend and colleague. I got to know Peter better when he began his role as Executive Director of the Southern California Veterinary Medical Association (SCVMA). During this period, I had multiple opportunities to sit and talk with Peter about the profession, where it was going, and how people could thrive while costs were rising, office visits were slowing, and practice models were changing. It was then that I recognized Peter's devotion to the professionals he served. As he said in this book, "you can be a good veterinarian and a good businessperson. In fact, you can be a better veterinarian if you are a good businessperson because you will have the ability to focus on the patient." Peter has seen most sides of small-animal practice and business. **He lectures on the subject with verve for having his colleagues institute many of the opportunities open to them.** His end game is to improve the profession and to see his colleagues enjoy practicing.

Business management is an important part of the practice of veterinary medicine, and **Peter has done much to serve the community that strives to implement good practice.**

Stephen Ettinger, DVM, DACVIM

I have known Dr. Peter Weinstein for more than twenty years. He is a forward-thinking innovator who deserves praise from the veterinary profession. His tireless work in guiding organized veterinary medicine is commendable. **This book should take center stage by all veterinary professionals, because it unlocks the thinking and provides the guidance needed to take the profession to new heights.**

Darin Nelson, Senior VP, Trupanion Pet Insurance,
www.trupanion.com

What can I say about Dr. Peter Weinstein that isn't obvious by reading this incredible new book? I have known Peter for many years as a colleague and a friend. I can still remember when he came to town. I didn't take a lot of interest initially because I was too busy working twelve-hour days and catching naps on my desk at the animal hospital. However, when Peter opened up a veterinary hospital very close to mine, I did take notice. Democracy, capitalism, and the American way work great as long as there is no direct competition to cloud your overworked, sleep-deprived thoughts. Despite it all, I came to realize that Peter was too smart, too compassionate, too professionally supportive, and too non-competitive to not like and respect.

The book makes you think. Working as the chief of staff of a large, prestigious small-animal hospital, I bought my first house because I couldn't afford my apartment (some kind of tax thing). I bought the veterinary practice because I couldn't afford the home mortgage on my salary. The picture was clear as mud. Like everyone else, I knew nothing about running a business, much less a veterinary hospital. Despite being extremely driven to succeed, my good fortune centered on surrounding myself with good people (manager, accountant, practice management consultant, tax advisor, business lawyer) who knew much more than I did. In the days of creative financing, my e-seizure was the stark reality that if the business didn't grow 25 percent the first year, my partner and I were doomed.

One benefit of this book is that hopefully the next generation will not have to learn everything the hard way. The alternating chapters by Gerber and Weinstein create an exciting format. **Read it, absorb what you can, and act. Life is short; don't waste it.**

Charles Acton, D.V.M., past Diplomate, ABVP,
Owner, Laguna Hills Animal Hospital, www.lagunahillsanimalhospital.com

I have always been an advocate for doing research and reading outside the veterinary programs and paradigms. I first met Peter when he was in his Master's study, and assisted his search for a new perspective. This book has now brought the outside in. Michael Gerber is in his usual rare form (E-Myth perspective), and Peter has again excelled in putting the rubber onto the road in a reasonable manner, for better traction by the veterinary practice reader. **I consider this book as a landmark synergy effort and a must-read for every practice owner/manager/leader.**

Thomas E. Catanzaro, DVM, MHA, LFACHE, Diplomate,
American College of Healthcare Executives; CEO,
Veterinary Consulting International

This is the latest in a series of business-specific books spawned from the original book, *The E-Myth: Why Most Businesses Don't Work and What to Do About It*, first published more than 25 years ago. The original E-Myth was a game changer, and among the first to focus on a business at the organism level, recognizing the dynamic interaction of the various components and how their synergy promotes long-term success and satisfaction. If you've read any of Mr. Gerber's previous books you'll recognized a familiar style, with a storyline serving as the scaffolding for the business principles that follow.

This veterinary version will stimulate you to think about why and how you provide services to your patients and their owners. **It promises generous rewards (in financial success *and* in personal satisfaction) for those who embrace the concepts shared in the book.**

The original E-Myth and this new addition for veterinary medicine defines a more successful management/leadership style based on a systems approach. His co-author has broad experience and insights to help the veterinarian-reader to specifically apply the book's principles to the veterinary profession.

The book outlines key areas for management/leadership effort, fosters change, and encourages purposeful action. The authors' goals are clear: veterinarians who want more success and satisfaction need to take control—we "get what we earn." It seems self-evident that change requires change. Approached right, it can be rejuvenating and an improved future is achievable for those willing to pursue it.

This is a worthy read if you're ready to take the action necessary to transform your practice to provide more success *and* satisfaction for your patients, their owners, your staff, your associates . . . and for you.

Don Klingborg, DVM, Associate Dean Emeritus,
UC Davis School of Veterinary Medicine

I've known Peter for many years now, and he's always doing his best for our profession. Once again he nails it right here! An awesome book—**and about time that someone told the truth about our industry.**

Diederik Gelderman, BVSc, MVS
Turbo Charge Your Practice, www.turbochargeyourpractice.com

Magnificent. Timely. Insightful. Revealing. Duh. These were just a few of the words that came to mind as I progressed through the book. The authors cleverly weave their experiences in a way that creates an "*aha*" moment for the reader who is thinking about the business of veterinary medicine or immersed in it. **With all of the recent professional focus on the veterinary economy, this book may be just what the doctor ordered.** It is, at a minimum, a significant resource to those practitioners who desire to be medically proficient and successful.

Phillip D. Nelson, DVM, PhD, Dean,
College of Veterinary Medicine, Western University of Health Science

Dr. Weinstein has accurately and concisely identified the unparalleled challenges that today's veterinarians and practice owners face each day in practice. Peter has made a compelling case in *The E-Myth Veterinarian* that veterinarians can manage the tension between ethics and economics by thinking differently—evolving from technicians who do it, do it, do it, to entrepreneurs who can create value for their practice, their staff, their clients, and ultimately the patients they have been trained to care for. **A must-read for any veterinary professional who cares passionately about this profession.**

Dr. Edward and Pamela Cole, Practice Owners, Irvine, CA

Dr. Peter Weinstein has been coaching, teaching, and facilitating excellence and innovation in veterinary practice for a long time. His personal support and guidance have been very instrumental for the success of my professional life. I own two successful veterinary hospitals in Southern California and I work on the businesses two days a week. I see patients and perform surgery one to two days a week as well, except for the eight or more weeks I travel with my family. *The E-Myth Veterinarian* is **the best guide that I have ever read to having a happy, balanced, and successful professional career.** This book should be required reading for every veterinary student (and veterinarian) in the country.

Jeff Horner, DVM, Diplomate, ABVP, Canine and Feline, Orange, CA

If anyone knows how to run veterinary medicine as a business and not a passion that you hope works, it is Peter. For years he has discussed, lectured, and written about basics changes, made on a consistent basis, that a veterinary hospital would flourish. **For any hospital that is ready to stop the chaos and and embrace sanity, this book is a must-read for you.**

Kelly Baltzell, M.A., CEO,
Beyond Indigo Pets/Equine, www.beyondindigo.com

As a veterinary business attorney, I advise my clients who are either starting a new veterinary practice, purchasing an existing practice, or buying into a veterinary practice as a partner that they must focus on how they are going to successfully build their practice to establish an exit strategy—even at the time of the start-up or purchase. *The E-Myth Veterinarian* **contains concepts that all veterinary practice owners, or individuals contemplating practice ownership, need to consider in order to achieve their ownership goals and to create a successful exit strategy.** It is impossible to read *The E-Myth Veterinarian* and not be impacted in some way. This is a hands-on, real-world analysis that I recommend all practice owners read.

Edward J. Guiducci, Esq.,
Guiducci & Guiducci PC, Arvada, Colorado

If anybody could bring transformation to how we operate veterinary practices, it's Peter Weinstein and Michael Gerber. Their insights are clear and practical, giving practitioners and managers a blueprint for how to build a great veterinary practice. Peter Weinstein's experiences and insights are beautifully laced between Michael Gerber's profound truths; the result is a book you'll have a hard time putting down.

This is not a book you read once. The first read is an appetizer for going back again and again.

As Peter Weinstein shares his veterinary practice struggles, I can relate to everything he went through along the way. I felt like he was in my practice taking notes. He just happens to have the courage to share these challenges and experiences with the world.

This book may have a bigger influence on shaping young veterinarians than any textbook on their shelves. The insights shared by Peter Weinstein and Michael Gerber are refreshing and clearly destined to impact the future of the profession, restoring joy back into the practice of veterinary medicine for many.

After reading most of this book in a single weekend, I quickly imagined how I had to take my leadership team through this powerful book. Peter and Michael hit the nail on the head with this book.

David Grant, DVM
President, Animal Care Technologies (ACT)

Every time I encounter Dr. Weinstein, I learn something new and exciting about veterinary medicine or veterinary management. This book is no exception! He and Michael Gerber have produced a game changer for those veterinarians who continue to work feverishly as clinicians, visionaries, financiers, managers, and owners. When the book is available for purchase, I plan to buy copies for the dozen or so members of our hospital leadership team. Not only do the authors dispense incredibly valuable information and advice for small business owners, but this text will be extremely helpful to managers at all levels of veterinary practice as they pause long enough to think about the systems that their hospitals need to function, whether or not the owner or manager is physically present. *The E-Myth Veterinarian* is **a refreshing, energizing resource that should be on every veterinary hospital owner's or manager's bookshelf.**

Jon Cunnington, MBA, CVPM, Hospital Administrator,
VCA Loomis Basin Veterinary Clinic

Dr. Weinstein's enthusiasm, dedication, and application of Michael Gerber's multidisciplinary principles illustrate the benefits of an organization being bigger than any one individual. Michael again has created a roadmap to a life-changing event for entrepreneurs willing to embrace meaningful change. Hence, *The E-Myth Veterinarian* **is a must-read for those in pursuit of their "Preferred Futures".**

Craig J. Mohnacky, DVM, Mohnacky Learning Systems

The E-Myth Veterinarian reads like a sit-down, one-on-one conversation with Dr. Peter Weinstein, whom, if you have ever had the pleasure to experience, you know what a knowledgeable and insightful person he is. Likewise, *The E-Myth Veterinarian* **will give you valuable insights you would not likely come to on your own.** This is a must-read for every veterinarian, to-be veterinarian, and everyone who loves and supports them.

Philip R. Homsey II, Esq.

Will the veterinary profession finally listen to the truth? Continue to work for the practice or buy this essential book, read, read, read, and then embrace its proven philosophy. Let your practice work for you and enjoy your new freedom.

Finally, an amazing ray of sunshine for a stubborn profession.

Required reading for every veterinarian, veterinary student, technician, manager, and staff to help you develop an amazing practice, plus a more enjoyable life. The practice will work for you, and you will no longer be working for the practice.

Honest, proven methods guaranteed to change your life.

Michael and Peter present a book to make your practice work for you and shatter the chains binding you to your practice.

A cookbook to your practice freedom and your lost life.

Steven M. Orme, DVM

I want to take this opportunity to thank Peter for his mention of me as a mentor. In truth, this is a classic example of the student becoming the teacher. Peter's entire life as a veterinarian has been dedicated to the service of his patients, clients, employers, practice, family, community, and our profession. As an illustration of this dedication, *The E-Myth Veterinarian* **will provide a valuable guide as we strive to balance our personal and professional lives,** while dealing with the challenges of an ever-changing world.

John Hamil, DVM

Dr. Weinstein has dedicated his career to veterinary medicine and is passionate about ensuring the successful ownership of veterinary practices by veterinarians. In working with Peter, I have seen his positive impact on the lives of veterinarians; **his vision has helped veterinarians recognize both professional and personal success through practice ownership.** *The E Myth Veterinarian* is a compilation of key insights and experiences gained over his career and is an excellent tool for anyone who wants to learn to run a successful veterinary practice.

Travis York, Managing Director,
Calico Financial

Michael's work has been an inspiration to us. **His books have helped us get free from the out-of-control life that we once had. His no-nonsense approach kept us focused on our ultimate aim rather than day-to-day stresses. He has helped take our business to levels we couldn't have imagined possible.** In the Dreaming Room™ made us totally re-evaluate how we thought about our business and our life. We have now redesigned our life so we can manifest the dreams we unearthed in Michael's Dreaming Room™.

Jo and Steve Davison, founders, The Spinal Health Clinic Chiropractic Group and www.your-dream-life.com

Michael Gerber's *The E-Myth* is one of only four books I recommend as required reading. **For those looking to start and build a business of their own, this is the man who has coached more successful entrepreneurs than the next ten gurus combined.**

Timothy Ferris, #1 *New York Times* best-selling author, *The 4-Hour Workweek*

Everyone needs a mentor, someone who tells it like it is, holds you accountable, and shows you your good, bad, and ugly. For millions of small-business owners, Michael Gerber is that person. Let Michael be your mentor and you are in for a kick in the pants, the ride of a lifetime.

John Jantsch, author, *Duct Tape Marketing*

Michael Gerber's strategies in *The E-Myth* were instrumental in building my company from two employees to a global organization; I can't wait to see how applying the strategies from *Awakening the Entrepreneur Within* will affect its growth!

Dr. Ivan Misner, founder and chairman, BNI; author, *Masters of Sales*

Michael Gerber's gift to isolate the issues and present simple, direct, business-changing solutions shines bright with *Awakening the Entrepreneur Within*. **If you're interested in developing an entrepreneurial vision and plan that inspires others to action, buy this book, read it, and apply the processes Gerber brilliantly defines.**

Tim Templeton, author, *The Referral of a Lifetime*

Michael Gerber is a master instructor and a leader's leader. As a combat F-15 fighter pilot, I had to navigate complex missions with life-and-death consequences, but until I read *The E-Myth* and met Michael Gerber, my transition to the world of small business was a nightmare with no real flight plan. **The hands-on, practical magic of Michael's turnkey systems magnified by the raw power of his keen insight and wisdom have changed my life forever.**

Steve Olds, CEO, www.stratworx.com

Michael Gerber truly, truly understands what it takes to be a successful practicing entrepreneur and business owner. He has demonstrated to me over six years of working with him that for those who stay the course and learn much more than just "how to work on their business and not in it," then they will reap rich rewards. **I finally franchised my business, and the key to unlocking this kind of potential in any business is the teaching of Michael's work.**

Chris Owen, marketing director, Royal Armouries (International) PLC

Because of Michael Gerber, I transformed my twenty-four-hour-a-day, seven-day-a-week job (also called a small business) into a multimillion-dollar turnkey business. This in turn set the foundation for my worldwide training firm. **I am living my dream because of Michael Gerber.**

Howard Partridge, Phenomenal Products Inc.

Michael Gerber is an outrageous revolutionary who is changing the way the world does business. **He dares you to commit to your grandest dreams and then shows you how to make the impossible a reality. If you let him, this man will change your life.**

Fiona Fallon, founder, Divine and The Bottom Line

Michael Gerber is a truly remarkable man. His steady openness of mind and ability to get to the deeper level continue to be an inspiration and encouragement to me. **He seems to always ask that one question that forces the new perspective to break open, and he approaches the new coming method in a fearless way.**

Rabbi Levi Cunin, Chabad of Malibu

Michael Gerber is a genius. Every successful business person I meet has read Michael Gerber, refers to Michael Gerber, and lives by his words. You just can't get enough of Michael Gerber. **He has the innate (and rare) ability to tap into one's soul, look deeply, and tell you what you need to hear. And then, he inspires you and equips you with the tools to get it done.**

Pauline O'Malley, CEO, TheRevenueBuilder

When asked "Who was the most influential person in your life?" I am one of the thousands who don't hesitate to say "Michael E. Gerber." **Michael helped transform me from someone dreaming of retirement to someone dreaming of working until age one hundred.** This awakening is the predictable outcome of anyone reading Michael's new book.

Thomas O. Bardeen

Michael Gerber is an incredible business philosopher, guru, perhaps even a seer. He has an amazing intuition, which allows him to see in an instant what everybody else is missing; he sees opportunity everywhere. **While I was in the Dreaming Room™, Michael gave me the gift of seeing through the eyes of an awakened entrepreneur, and instantly my business changed from a regional success to serving clients on four continents.**

Keith G. Schiehl, president, Rent-a-Geek Computer Services

Michael Gerber forced me to think big, think real, and gave me the support network to make it happen. A new wave of entrepreneurs is rising, much in thanks to his amazing efforts and very practical approach to doing business.

Christian Kessner, founder, Higher Ground Retreats and Events

Michael Gerber is among the very few who truly understand entrepreneurship and small business. While others talk about these topics in the form of theories, methodologies, processes, and so on, Michael goes to the heart of the issues. **Whenever Michael writes about entrepreneurship, soak it in, as it is not only good for your business, but great for your soul.** His words will help you to keep your passion and balance while sailing through the uncertain sea of entrepreneurship.

Raymond Yeh, co-author, *The Art of Business*

Michael's understanding of entrepreneurship and small-business management has been a difference maker for countless businesses, including Infusion Software. **His insights into the entrepreneurial process of building a business are a must-read for every small-business owner.** The vision, clarity, and leadership that came out of our Dreaming Room™ experience were just what our company needed to recognize our potential and motivate the whole company to achieve it.

Clate Mask, president and CEO, Infusion Software

The Dreaming Room™ experience was literally life-changing for us. **Within months, we were able to start our foundation and make several television appearances owing to his teachings.** He has an incredible charisma, which is priceless, but above all Michael Gerber awakens passion from within, enabling you to take action with dramatic results . . . starting today!

Shona and Shaun Carcary
Trinity Property Investments Inc., Home Vestors franchises

I thought *E-Myth* was an awkward name! What could this book do for me? **But when I finally got to reading it . . . it was what I was looking for all along.** Then, to top it off, I took a twenty-seven-hour trip to San Diego just to attend the Dreaming Room™, where Michael touched my heart, my mind, and my soul.

Helmi Natto, president, Eye 2 Eye Optics, Saudi Arabia

I attended In the Dreaming Room™ and was challenged by Michael Gerber to "Go out and do what's impossible." So I did; **I became an author and international speaker and used Michael's principles to create a world-class company that will change and save lives all over the world.**

Dr. Don Kennedy, MBA; author, *5 AM & Already Behind*, www.bahbits.com

I went to the Dreaming Room™ to have Michael Gerber fix my business. He talked about Dreaming. What was this Dreaming? I was too busy working! Too busy being miserable, angry, frustrated, behind in what I was trying to accomplish. And losing everything I was working for. **Then Michael Gerber woke up the dreamer in me and remade my life and my business.**

Pat Doorn, president, Mountain View Electric Ltd.

The E Myth Veterinarian

Why Most Veterinary Practices Don't Work and What to Do About It

MICHAEL E. GERBER

PETER WEINSTEIN, DVM

PRODIGY
BUSINESS BOOKS

Published by
Prodigy Business Books, Inc., Carlsbad, California.

Production Team
Patricia Beaulieu, COO, Prodigy Business Books, Inc.; Meredith Watkins, editor, Green Sparrow Literary Services; Erich Broesel, cover designer, BroeselDesign, Inc.; Nancy Ratkiewich, book production, njr productions; Jeff Kassebaum, Michael E. Gerber author photographer, Jeff Kassebaum and Co.; George Toland, Peter Weinstein co-author photographer, Sixth Rib Photography

For general information on other products and services, please visit the website: www.michaelegerber.com.

ISBN 978-1-61835-033-6 (cloth)
ISBN 978-1-61835-034-3 (audio)
ISBN 978-1-61835-035-0 (e-book)

Printed in the United States of America

10 9 8 7 6 5 4 3 2 1

To Luz Delia, whose heart expands mine,
whose soul inspires mine,
whose boldness reaches for the stars, thank you,
forever, for being, truly mine . . .

—Michael E. Gerber

CONTENTS

A WORD ABOUT THIS BOOK

Michael E. Gerber

My first E-Myth book was published in 1985. It was called *The E-Myth: Why Most Businesses Don't Work and What to Do About It*. Since that book, and the practice I created to provide business development services to its many readers, millions have read *The E-Myth* and the book that followed it, called *The E-Myth Revisited*, and tens of thousands have participated in our E-Myth Mastery programs.

The co-author of this book, Peter Weinstein, DVM, MBA, is one of my more enthusiastic readers, and as a direct result of his enthusiasm, his veterinary practice became one of those clients.

This book is two things: the product of my lifelong work conceiving, developing, and growing the E-Myth way into a business model that has been applied to every imaginable kind of practice in the world, as well as a product of Peter's extraordinary experience and success applying the E-Myth to the development of his equally extraordinary business.

So one day, while sitting with my muse, which I think of as my inner voice (and which many who know me think of as "here he goes again!"), I thought about the creation of an entire series of E-Myth Expert books. That series, including this book, would be co-authored by experts in every industry who had successfully applied my E-Myth principles to the extreme development of a sole proprietorship—an employer plus one—with the intent of growing it nationwide, and even worldwide, which is what Peter had in mind as he began to discover the almost infinite range of opportunities provided by thinking the E-Myth way.

Upon seeing the possibilities of this new idea, I immediately invited co-authors such as Peter to join me. He said, "Let's do it!" and so we did.

Welcome to *The E-Myth Veterinarian: Why Most Veterinary Practices Don't Work and What to Do About It*.

Read it, enjoy it, and let us—Peter and I—help you apply the E-Myth to the re-creation, development, and extreme growth of your veterinary practice into an enterprise that you can be justifiably proud of.

To your life, your wisdom, and the life and success of your patients, I wish you good reading.

—Michael E. Gerber
Co-Founder/Chairman
Michael E. Gerber Companies, Inc.
Carlsbad, California
www.michaelegerber.com/co-author

A NOTE FROM PETER

Peter Weinstein, DVM, MBA

As I write this I keep thinking, I feel the pain that the veterinary profession and veterinarians go through. My name is Dr. Peter Weinstein and I am a veterinarian. I was an associate, a practice owner, a consultant, and I held a plethora of other veterinary-related gigs. And although I don't presently see clients in exam rooms or visit with patients who lick my face or purr, so many of my friends and day-to-day contacts are active in the practice of veterinary medicine that I vicariously feel the pain that they feel. This book is my opportunity to help you relieve your pain!

Many of my closest friends know that I am a *huge* Bruce Springsteen fan. Many of his songs are about unfulfilled dreams, such as these words from *Badlands:*

> "*Talk about a dream,*
> *try to make it real.*
> *You wake up in the night,*
> *with a fear so real.*
> *Spend your life waiting,*
> *for a moment that just don't come.*
> *Well, don't waste your time waiting.*"

In fact, just like many of you, I thought that the great American dream of personal and professional success looked easy. Go to school, work hard, get your degree, go to professional school, get your degree, get a job, get mentored, go to the bank, get some money, open your own business, and make a lot of money. Simple?

Not!

In my teens, I dreamed of becoming a veterinarian. I was going to be a dog and cat doctor (I did have the equine surgeon dream for a little while), just like the veterinarians who I went to as a client and worked for as a volunteer, a kennel kid, a veterinary assistant, and a receptionist. And after a few attempts, I finally got into veterinary school.

I really don't think that many veterinarians entered veterinary school with any idea of what it was going to take to run a veterinary business. Thinking back to the University of Illinois in the mid-'80s, our business education was an elective taught in a small lecture theater in the large animal clinic. By video tape. With a speaker sitting down behind a desk. In black and white. Truly motivational. With that foundation in hand, I was ill-prepared to become a veterinary entrepreneur. And even though, we've come a long way since then, there are still very few who are prepared for the rigors of being a veterinary professional running a veterinary business.

In school you are taught how to be a good doctor. But that doesn't guarantee you will have a successful practice. Having a successful practice doesn't mean you will have a financially successful business. Having a financially successful business doesn't mean you will have a globally successful enterprise. In fact, when it comes to the veterinary field, it is deemed impossible to be a good doctor *and* a good businessperson. Veterinarians are supposed to be caring and compassionate individuals whose concerns about making money are secondary to their concerns about taking care of animals.

Let's dispel a rumor. You *can* be a good veterinarian and a good businessperson. In fact, you can be a better veterinarian if you are a good businessperson because you will have the ability to focus on the patient, while not worrying strictly about the pocketbook of their two-legged companion. In my experience, the veterinarians who have been great clinicians and have been able to balance that with being great business people, also seem to have the happiest clients, the happiest staff, and balanced lives.

I spent the first three years of my practice-owning life trying to balance it all. It wasn't working. The Great American Dream was the Great American Scream. There were times I wondered why it all looked so easy for some and was so frustrating for me. I was good at not letting anybody—my wife, my staff, my clients—know what I was going through. But I wasn't having fun, and the light I kept seeing at the end of the tunnel was a train.

And then, while attending a practice management continuing education program, I was exposed to the name Michael Gerber and his book, *The E-Myth*. I read the book over a few days. And reread it. Underlined. Dog-eared. And annotated.

Then, I had the chance to see and hear Michael Gerber speak. It was the gospel according to Michael and I was hooked. He made it sound so easy, I convinced myself I could do it too. So while going back to school to get my MBA and running my practice, I implemented many of the programs outlined in the book. My life was changed. My practice life was changed. And I realized that I wasn't working for a lunatic anymore; I was working for the person who was going to buy my practice. The lucky soul who would get an organized and systematized veterinary hospital. Both of us would benefit: myself as the seller and the other entity as the buyer.

I also knew then that I was going to be an advocate for the E-Myth model. Every opportunity that I had to write or speak, I would talk about the concepts, the programs, the processes, the operational efficiencies, and the systems that Michael had so profoundly identified. But most importantly, I learned it was imperative to get veterinarians to have a vision. A dream. A focus. A direction. So many of my colleagues go to work for the sake of going to work and to generate a paycheck. They truly don't have any idea of why they are doing what they are doing and why what they do intricately impacts their entire life. You, your business, and your family are so intimately intertwined that they all have a common blood supply. And that blood supply starts in you.

They say you make your own luck, and how I became a co-author of this book is one of those fortuitous situations. In

February 2014, I had the opportunity to speak at the Western Veterinary Conference. One of my talks delved into systems and I made the statement that, "*The E-Myth Revisited* is a mandatory read for anybody in the small business world." About a month later, I received a call from Michael E. Gerber's company while I was traveling in Seattle. I had no idea the reason for the call, but when Mr. Gerber's assistant asked to set up a call with *the* Michael Gerber, I was speechless. And as they say, the rest is history.

This book is a dream for me. It is the ability for me to put into writing the ideas, thoughts, beliefs, and concepts that have been wandering around my grey matter for more than 20 years. I can give back to my colleagues and provide some guidance to help many of them out of the wilderness where they have wandered all by themselves for forty years, four years, four months, or four days. You have the culmination of one of my dreams in your hands, or in your ear buds.

Take this opportunity to read the words of one of the most influential small business authors of the era. Think deeply about your practice. Is it all it can be? Are you getting all you want out of it? Are you sleeping well at night? Can you see ever being able to get out of the practice everything you put in? Finally, are you tired of just doing it, doing it, doing it, while working for a lunatic who has no idea of what he is doing, so he just keeps working?

Here's your chance to work toward your American Dream. Go for it!

—Peter Weinstein, DVM, MBA
President, PAW Consulting
3972 Barranca Parkway
Suite J-137
Irvine, CA 92606
peterweinsteindvm@gmail.com

PREFACE

Michael E. Gerber

I am not a veterinarian, though I have helped dozens of veterinarians reinvent their practices over the past thirty-five years.

I like to think of myself as a thinker, maybe even a dreamer. Yes, I like to *do* things. But before I jump in and get my hands dirty, I prefer to think through what I'm going to do and figure out the best way to do it. I imagine the impossible, dream big, and then try to figure out how the impossible can become the possible. After that, it's about how to turn the possible into reality.

Over the years, I've made it my business to study how things work and how people work—specifically, how things and people work best together to produce optimum results. That means creating an organization that can do great things and achieve more than any other organization can.

This book is about how to produce the best results as a real-world veterinarian in the development, expansion, and *liberation* of your practice. In the process, you will come to understand what veterinary practice—as a *business*—is, and what it isn't. If you keep focusing on what it isn't, you're destined for failure. But if you turn your sights on what it is, the tide will turn.

This book, intentionally small, is about big ideas. The topics we'll discuss in this book are the very issues that veterinarians face daily in their companies. You know what they are: money, management, patients, and many more. My aim is to help you begin the exciting process of totally transforming the way you do business. As such, I'm confident that *The E-Myth Veterinarian* could well be the most important book on veterinary practice as a business that you'll ever read.

Unlike other books on the market, my goal is not to tell you how to do the work you do. Instead, I want to share with you the E-Myth philosophy as a way to revolutionize the way you think about the work you do. I'm convinced that this new way of thinking is something veterinarians everywhere must adopt in order for their veterinary practices to flourish during these trying times. I call it strategic thinking, as opposed to tactical thinking.

In strategic thinking, also called systems thinking, you, the veterinarian, will begin to think about your entire practice—the broad scope of it—instead of focusing on its individual parts. You will begin to see the end game (perhaps for the first time) rather than just the day-to-day routine that's consuming you—the endless, draining work I call "doing it, doing it, doing it."

Understanding strategic thinking will enable you to create a practice that becomes a successful business, with the potential to flourish as an even more successful enterprise. But in order for you to accomplish this, your practice, your business, and certainly your enterprise must work apart from you instead of because of you.

The E-Myth philosophy defines a practice as a sole proprietorship, a business, or an enterprise, so you will see these designations used throughout the book. In some industries, a practice can also be called a practice or sole proprietorship. For the purposes of this book, my references to a practice refer to a sole proprietorship.

Accordingly, a practice is created and owned by a technician; a business is created and owned by a manager; and an enterprise is created and owned by an entrepreneur.

The E-Myth philosophy says that a highly successful veterinary practice can grow into a highly successful veterinary business, which, in turn, can become the foundation for an inordinately successful veterinary enterprise that runs smoothly and efficiently without the veterinarian having to be in the office for ten hours a day, six days a week.

So what is *The E-Myth*, exactly? The E-Myth is short for the Entrepreneurial Myth, which says that most businesses fail to fulfill

their potential because most people starting their own
are not entrepreneurs at all. They're actually what I call technicians suffering from an entrepreneurial seizure. When technicians suffering from an entrepreneurial seizure start a veterinary practice of their own, they almost always end up working themselves into a frenzy; their days are booked solid with appointments. These veterinarians are burning the candle at both ends, fueled by too much coffee and too little sleep, and most of the time, they can't even stop to think.

In short, the E-Myth says that most veterinarians don't own a true business—most own a job. They're doing it, doing it, doing it, hoping like hell to get some time off, but never figuring out how to get their business to run without them. And if your business doesn't run well without you, what happens when you can't be in two places at once? Ultimately, your practice will fail.

There are a number of prestigious schools throughout the world dedicated to teaching veterinary medicine. The problem is they fail to teach the business of it. And because no one is being taught how to run a practice as a business, some veterinarians find themselves having to close their doors every year. You could be a world-class expert in veterinary diagnosis and treatment, but when it comes to building a successful practice, all that specified knowledge matters exactly zilch.

The good news is that you don't have to be among the statistics of failure in the veterinary profession. The E-Myth philosophy I am about to share with you in this book has been successfully applied to thousands of veterinary practices just like yours, with extraordinary results.

The key to transforming your practice—and your life—is to grasp the profound difference between going to work on your business (systems thinker) and going to work in your business (tactical thinker). In other words, it's the difference between going to work on your business as an entrepreneur and going to work in your business as a veterinarian.

The two are not mutually exclusive. In fact, they are essential to each other. The problem with most veterinary practices is that the systems thinker—the entrepreneur—is completely absent. And so is the vision.

The E-Myth philosophy says that the key to transforming your practice into a successful enterprise is knowing how to transform yourself from successful veterinary technician into successful technician-manager-entrepreneur. In the process, everything you do in your veterinary practice will be transformed. The door is then open to turning it into what it should be—a practice, a business, and an enterprise of pure joy.

The E-Myth not only can work for you, it will work for you. In the process, it will give you an entirely new experience of your practice and beyond.

To your future and your life. Good reading.

—Michael E. Gerber
Co-Founder/Chairman
Michael E. Gerber Companies, Inc.
Carlsbad, California
www.michaelegerber.com/co-author

ACKNOWLEDGMENTS

Michael E. Gerber

As always, and never to be forgotten, there are those who give of themselves to make my work possible.

To my dearest and most forgiving partner, wife, friend, and co-founder, Luz Delia Gerber, whose love and commitment takes me to places I would often not go unaccompanied.

To Meredith Watkins, without your insightful edits and endless hours, we might never have made our many deadlines! To Erich Broesel, our stand-alone graphic designer and otherwise visual genius who supported the creation of all things visual that will forever be all things Gerber, we thank you, deeply, for your continuous contribution of things both temporal and eternal. To Trish Beaulieu, wow, you are splendid. And to Nancy Ratkiewich, whose work has been essential for you who are reading this.

To those many, many dreamers, thinkers, storytellers, and leaders, whose travels with me in The Dreaming Room™ have given me life, breath, and pleasure unanticipated before we met. To those many participants in my life (you know who you are), thank you for taking me seriously, and joining me in this exhilarating quest.

And, of course, to my co-authors, all of you, your genius, wisdom, intelligence, and wit have supplied me with a grand view of the world, which would never have been the same without you.

Love to all.

ACKNOWLEDGMENTS

Peter Weinstein, DVM, MBA

To my parents, who never tried to convince me to go to medical school and drove me, supported me, and believed in me when I had a hard time believing in myself.

This dream would never have been fulfilled without the support, understanding, and belief of my wife, Sharon. It was her nudge that motivated me to take on this project and her sacrifices that allowed me to get it done.

My kids, Brooke and Brianna, who wonder why Daddy is always working and hopefully have learned that you never give up on a dream.

For Tom Cat (Tom Catanzaro, DVM, DACHE) who believed in me enough to add me to his team and who is so far ahead of his time in his thinking that I am in awe. And to all of Tom Cat's kittens who helped me gain the confidence to want to change practices and the profession.

It is rare when you can acknowledge your mentors for their influence on your life. I'd like to recognize Drs. Arthur Kronfeld, Floyd Mann, and Charles Gauger who showed me the ropes when I was just a veterinarian wannabe. Dr. Steve Orme who took on a really green veterinarian and guided me, coaxed me, and motivated me and then became a great friend. Finally, Dr. John Hamil, a role model for the veterinary profession when it comes to being a true clinician by taking care of people and pets the right way, while always being an advocate for veterinary medicine. As a friend, mentor, and leader, there is no comparison.

And to the veterinary profession and my colleagues who motivate me, frustrate me, irritate me, believe in me, and support me through my various permutations. This is a work of passion dedicated to each and every one of you.

For caring and compassionate veterinary hospital teams who live in a world of chaos seeking some sanity, my dream is to make your world a more predictable place so that jobs become careers, and your passion to make a difference never wanes.

And to Michael Gerber, who provides a path for anybody, in any field, to find the light at the end of the tunnel. The E-Myth mindset has influenced more people than can ever be imagined and has transformed this technician into an entrepreneur who now looks forward to carrying the E-Myth banner into the veterinary profession.

INTRODUCTION

Michael E. Gerber

As I write this book, the aftermath of the recession and the slow economic recovery continue to take its toll on American businesses. Like any other industry, veterinary practices are not immune. Veterinarians all over the country are watching as finances are tight and pet owners must prioritize where their limited funds are spent.

Faced with a struggling economy and tighter household finances, many veterinarians I've met are asking themselves, "Why did I ever become a veterinarian in the first place?"

And it isn't just a money problem. After thirty-five years of working with small businesses, many of them veterinary practices, I'm convinced that the dissatisfaction experienced by countless veterinarians is not just about money. To be frank, the recession doesn't deserve all the blame, either. While the financial crisis our country faced certainly hasn't made things any better, the problem started long before the economy tanked. Let's dig a little deeper. Let's go back to school.

Can you remember that far back? Whichever university or college of veterinary medicine you attended, you probably had some great teachers who helped you become the fine veterinarian you are. These schools excel at teaching veterinary medicine; they'll teach you everything you need to know about diagnosis, treatment, and care of your patients, animal and human. But what they *don't* teach is the consummate skill set needed to be a successful veterinarian, and they certainly don't teach what it takes to build a successful veterinary practice.

Obviously, something is seriously wrong. The education that veterinarians receive in school doesn't go far enough, deep enough, broad enough. Veterinary programs don't teach you how to relate to the *enterprise* or to the *business* of veterinary practice; they only teach you how to relate to the *practice* of veterinary medicine. In other words, they merely teach you how to be an *effective* rather than a *successful* veterinarian. Last time I checked, they weren't offering degrees in success. That's why most veterinarians are effective, but few are successful.

Although a successful veterinarian must be effective, an effective veterinarian does not have to be—and in most cases isn't—successful.

An effective veterinarian is capable of executing his or her duties with as much certainty and professionalism as possible.

A successful veterinarian, on the other hand, works balanced hours, has little stress, enjoys rich and rewarding relationships with friends and family, and has an economic life that is diverse, fulfilling, and shows a continuous return on investment.

A successful veterinarian finds time and ways to give back to the community but at little cost to his or her sense of ease.

A successful veterinarian is a leader, not simply someone who teaches novices veterinary medicine, but a sage; a rich person (in the broadest sense of the word); a strong father, mother, wife, or husband; a friend, teacher, mentor, and spiritually grounded human being; and a person who can see clearly into all aspects of what it means to lead a fulfilling life.

So let's go back to the original question. Why did you become a veterinarian? Were you striving to just be an effective one, or did you dream about real and resounding success?

I don't know how you've answered that question in the past, but I am confident that once you understand the strategic thinking laid out in this book, you will answer it differently in the future.

If the ideas here are going to be of value to you, it's critical that you begin to look at yourself in a different, more productive way.

I am suggesting that you go beyond the mere technical aspects of your daily job as a veterinarian and begin instead to think strategically about your veterinary practice as both a business and an enterprise.

I often say that most *companies* don't work—the people who own them do. In other words, most veterinary practices are jobs for the veterinarians who own them. Does this sound familiar? The veterinarian, overcome by an entrepreneurial seizure, has started his or her own practice, become his or her own boss, and now works for a lunatic!

The result: the veterinarian is running out of time, patience, and ultimately money. Not to mention paying the worst price anyone can pay for the inability to understand what a true practice is, what a true business is, and what a true enterprise is—the price of his or her life.

In this book I'm going to make the case for why you should think differently about what you do and why you do it. It isn't just the future of your veterinary practice that hangs in the balance. It's the future of your life.

The E-Myth Veterinarian is an exciting departure from my other sole-authored books. In this book, an expert—a successful veterinarian who has successfully applied the E-Myth to the development of his veterinary practice—is sharing his secrets about how he achieved extraordinary results using the E-Myth paradigm. In addition to the time-tested E-Myth strategies and systems I'll be sharing with you, you'll benefit from the wisdom, guidance, and practical tips provided by a legion of veterinarians who've been in your shoes.

The problems that afflict veterinary practices today don't only exist in the field of veterinary medicine; the same problems are confronting every organization of every size, in every industry in every country in the world. *The E-Myth Veterinarian* is next in a new series of E-Myth Expert books that will serve as a launching pad for Michael E. Gerber Partners™ to bring a legacy of expertise to small, struggling businesses in *all* industries. This series will offer an exciting opportunity to understand and apply the significance of E-Myth methodology in both theory and practice to businesses in need of development and growth.

The E-Myth says that only by conducting your *business* in a truly innovative and independent way will you ever realize the unmatched joy that comes from creating a truly independent business, a business that works *without* you rather than *because* of you.

The E-Myth says that it is only by learning the difference between the work of a *business* and the business of *work* that veterinarians will be freed from the predictable and often overwhelming tyranny of the unprofitable, unproductive routine that consumes them on a daily basis.

The E-Myth says that what will make the ultimate difference between the success or failure of your veterinary practice is first and foremost how you think about your business, as opposed to how hard you work in it.

So, let's think it through together. Let's think about those things—work, patients, money, time—that dominate the world of veterinarians everywhere.

Let's talk about planning. About growth. About management. About getting a life!

Let's think about improving your and your family's life through the development of an extraordinary practice. About getting the life you've always dreamed of but never thought you could actually have.

Envision the future you want, and the future is yours.

CHAPTER

1

The Story of Steve and Peggy

Michael E. Gerber

You leave home to seek your fortune and, when you get it, you go home and share it with your family.

—Anita Baker

Every business is a family business. To ignore this truth is to court disaster.

This is true whether or not family members actually work in the business. Whatever their relationship with the business, every member of a veterinarian's family will be greatly affected by the decisions a veterinarian makes about the business. There's just no way around it.

Unfortunately, like most businessmen, veterinarians tend to compartmentalize their lives. They view their business as a profession—what they do—and therefore it's none of their family's business.

"This has nothing to do with you," says the veterinarian to his wife, with blind conviction. "I leave work at the office and family at home."

And with equal conviction, I say, "Not true!"

In actuality, your family and veterinary practice are inextricably linked to one another. What's happening in your practice is also happening at home. Consider the following and ask yourself if each is true:

- If you're angry at work, you're also angry at home.
- If you're out of control at your veterinary practice, you're equally out of control at home.
- If you're having trouble with money in your practice, you're also having trouble with money at home.
- If you have communication problems in your practice, you're also having communication problems at home.
- If you don't trust in your practice, you don't trust at home.
- If you're secretive in your practice, you're equally secretive at home.

And you're paying a huge price for it!

The truth is that your practice and your family are one—and you're the link. Or you should be. Because if you try to keep your practice and your family apart, if your practice and your family are strangers, you will effectively create two separate worlds that can never wholeheartedly serve each other. Two worlds that split each other apart.

Let me tell you the story of Steve and Peggy Walsh.

The Walshes met in college. They were partners in a study club for a chemistry class—Steve a veterinary student and Peggy in nursing. When their discussions started to wander beyond inorganic compounds and Bunsen burners and into their personal lives, they discovered they had a lot in common. By the end of the course, they weren't just talking in class; they were talking on the phone every night . . . and not about chemistry class.

Steve thought Peggy was absolutely brilliant, and Peggy considered Steve the most passionate man she knew. It wasn't long before they were engaged and planning their future together. A week after graduation, they were married in a lovely garden ceremony in Peggy's childhood home.

While Steve studied veterinary medicine at a prestigious college, Peggy entered a nursing Masters program nearby. Over the next few years, the couple worked hard to keep their finances afloat. They worked long hours and studied constantly; they were often exhausted and struggled to make ends meet. But through it all, they were committed to what they were doing and to each other.

After graduating, Steve became a veterinarian in a busy practice, while Peggy began working at a large hospital nearby. Soon afterward, the couple had their first son, and Peggy decided to take some time off to be with him. Those were good years. Steve and Peggy loved each other very much, were active members in their church, participated in community organizations, and spent quality time together. The Walshes considered themselves one of the most fortunate families they knew.

But work became troublesome. Steve grew increasingly frustrated with the way the practice was run. "I want to go into business for myself," he announced one night at the dinner table. "I want to start my own practice."

Steve and Peggy spent many nights talking about the move. Was it something they could afford? Did Steve really have the skills necessary to make a veterinary practice a success? Were there enough patients and deals to go around? What impact would such a move have on Peggy's career at the local hospital, their lifestyle, their son, their relationship? They asked all the questions they thought they needed to answer before Steve went into business for himself . . . but they never really drew up a concrete plan.

Finally, tired of talking and confident that he could handle whatever he might face, Steve committed to starting his own veterinary practice. Because she loved and supported him, Peggy agreed, offering her own commitment to help in any way she could. So Steve quit his job, took out a second mortgage on their home, and leased a small office nearby.

In the beginning, things went well. A building boom had hit the town, and new families were pouring into the area. Steve had no trouble getting new patients. His practice expanded, quickly outgrowing his office.

Within a year, Steve had employed an office manager, Clarissa, to run the front desk and handle the administrative side of the business. He also hired a bookkeeper, Tim, to handle the finances. Steve was ecstatic with the progress his young practice had made. He celebrated by taking his wife and son on vacation to Italy.

Of course, managing a business was more complicated and time-consuming than working for someone else. Steve not only supervised all the jobs Clarissa and Tim did, but also was continually looking for work to keep everyone busy. When he wasn't scanning veterinary journals to stay abreast of what was going on in the field or attending industry events to stay current, he was going to the bank, wading through patient paperwork, or speaking with mortgage companies (which usually degenerated into arguing with mortgage companies). He also found himself spending more and more time on the telephone dealing with patient complaints and nurturing relationships.

As the months went by and more and more patients came through the door, Steve had to spend even more time just trying to keep his head above water.

By the end of its second year, the practice, now employing two full-time and two part-time people, had moved to a larger office downtown. The demands on Steve's time had grown with the practice.

He began leaving home earlier in the morning and returning later at night. He drank more. He rarely saw his son anymore. For the most part, Steve was resigned to the problem. He saw the hard work as essential to building the "sweat equity" he had long heard about.

Money was also becoming a problem for Steve. Although the practice was growing like crazy, money always seemed scarce when it was really needed.

When Steve had worked for somebody else, he had been paid twice a month. In his own practice, he often had to wait—sometimes for months for patients to pay off a large procedure. Of course, no matter how slowly Steve got paid, he still had to pay his people. This became a relentless problem. Steve often felt like a juggler dancing on a tightrope. A fire burned in his stomach day and night.

To make matters worse, Steve began to feel that Peggy was insensitive to his troubles. Not that he often talked to his wife about the practice. "Business is business" was Steve's mantra. "It's my responsibility to handle things at the office and Peggy's responsibility to take care of her own job and the family."

Peggy was working late hours at the hospital, and they'd brought in a nanny to help with their son. Steve couldn't help but notice that his wife seemed resentful, and her apparent lack of understanding baffled him. Didn't she see that he had a practice to take care of? That he was doing it all for his family? Apparently not.

As time went on, Steve became even more consumed and frustrated by his practice. When he went off on his own, he remembered saying, "I don't like people telling me what to do." But people were still telling him what to do.

Not surprisingly, Peggy grew more frustrated by her husband's lack of communication. She cut back on her own hours at the hospital to focus on their family, but her husband still never seemed to be around. Their relationship grew tense and strained. The rare moments they were together were more often than not peppered by long silences—a far cry from the heartfelt conversations that had characterized their relationship's early days, when they'd talk into the wee hours of the morning.

Meanwhile, Tim, the bookkeeper, was also becoming a problem for Steve. Tim never seemed to have the financial information Steve needed to make decisions about payroll, billing, and general operating expenses, let alone how much money was available for Steve and Peggy's living expenses.

When questioned, Tim would shift his gaze to his feet and say, "Listen, Steve, I've got a lot more to do around here than you can imagine. It'll take a little more time. Just don't press me, okay?"

Overwhelmed by his own work, Steve usually backed off. The last thing Steve wanted was to upset Tim and have to do the books himself. He could also empathize with what Tim was going through, given the practice's growth over the past year.

Late at night in his office, Steve would sometimes recall his first years out of school. He missed the simple life he and his family had shared. Then, as quickly as the thoughts came, they would vanish. He had work to do and no time for daydreaming. "Having my own practice is a great thing," he would remind himself. "I simply have to apply myself, as I did in school, and get on with the job. I have to work as hard as I always have when something needed to get done."

Steve began to live most of his life inside his head. He began to distrust his people. They never seemed to work hard enough or to care about his practice as much as he did. If he wanted to go get something done, he usually had to do it himself.

Then one day, the office manager, Clarissa, quit in a huff, frustrated by the amount of work that her boss was demanding of her. Steve was left with a desk full of papers and a telephone that wouldn't stop ringing.

Clueless about the work Clarissa had done, Steve was overwhelmed by having to pick up the pieces of a job he didn't understand. His world turned upside down. He felt like a stranger in his own practice.

Why had he been such a fool? Why hadn't he taken the time to learn what Clarissa did in the office? Why had he waited until now?

Ever the trouper, Steve plowed into Clarissa's job with everything he could muster. What he found shocked him. Clarissa's work space was a disaster area! Her desk drawers were a jumble of papers, coins, pens, pencils, rubber bands, envelopes, business cards, fee slips, eye drops, and candy.

"What was she thinking?" Steve raged.

When he got home that night, even later than usual, he got into a shouting match with Peggy. He settled it by storming out of the house to get a drink. Didn't anybody understand him? Didn't anybody care what he was going through?

He returned home only when he was sure Peggy was asleep. He slept on the couch and left early in the morning, before anyone was awake. He was in no mood for questions or arguments. When Steve got to his office the next morning, he immediately headed for the break room, where he could put his head down to soothe his throbbing headache.

What lessons can we draw from Steve and Peggy's story? I've said it once and I'll say it again: Every business is a family business. Your business profoundly touches all members of your family, even if they never set foot inside your office. Every business either gives to the family or takes from the family, just as individual family members do.

If the business takes more than it gives, the family is always the first to pay the price.

In order for Steve to free himself from the prison he created, he would first have to admit his vulnerability. He would have to confess to himself and his family that he really didn't know enough about his own practice and how to grow it.

Steve tried to do it all himself. Had he succeeded, had the practice supported his family in the style he imagined, he would have burst with pride. Instead, Steve unwittingly isolated himself, thereby achieving the exact opposite of what he sought.

He destroyed his life—and his family's life along with it.

Repeat after me: Every business is a family business.

Are you like Steve? I believe that all veterinarians share a common soul with him. You must learn that a business is only a business. It is not your life. But it is also true that your business can have a profoundly negative impact on your life unless you learn how to do it differently than most veterinarians do it—and definitely differently than Steve did it.

Steve's veterinary practice could have served his and his family's life. But for that to happen, he would have had to learn how to master his practice in a way that was completely foreign to him.

Instead, Steve's practice consumed him. Because he lacked a true understanding of the essential strategic thinking that would have allowed him to create something unique, Steve and his family were doomed from day one.

This book contains the secrets that Steve should have known. If you follow in Steve's footsteps, prepare to have your life and business fall apart. But if you apply the principles we'll discuss here, you can avoid a similar fate.

Let's start with the subject of money. But, before we do, let's learn the veterinarian's view about the story I just told you. Let's talk about Peter's journey . . . and yours. ✤

CHAPTER
2

Been There, Done That

Peter Weinstein, DVM, MBA

You only have control over three things in your life—the thoughts you think, the images you visualize and the actions you take.

—Jack Canfield

I was a technician who had an entrepreneurial seizure, and this is my story. Maybe you'll see a little bit of yours in mine, too.

As a kid, while most of my friends wanted to be doctors or lawyers or engineers, I wanted to be a veterinarian. In spite of valiant efforts by guidance counselors to change my mind, I doggedly pursued my passion.

At age fifteen, I started volunteering at the veterinary hospital where we brought our cats. What started out as a position walking dogs and cleaning cages progressed to more and more involvement until eventually I was earning a paycheck. While observing my first mentors, Drs. Kronfeld and Mann at Port Washington Animal Hospital, I noticed what they could do for the animals. . .and the people. I also recognized the success they seemed to enjoy in their chosen path. But how they became successful—the business of being a veterinarian—was the farthest thing from my mind. I just knew I wanted to take care of animals.

Until now, this story parallels that of many veterinarians. You entered veterinary medicine to make a difference in the animal world—and the people world, too. Did you ever think about the business of veterinary medicine as you were laboring to get into veterinary school?

Once we cleared the hurdle of veterinary school admission, our professional education became all about systems: respiratory, cardiovascular, renal, reproductive, musculoskeletal, etc. We examined how organ systems all integrate together to make a living entity thrive and survive. We learned that if any system fails, all systems may eventually fail. And we even got down to the molecular level to understand the smallest feedback mechanisms, interactive communication, and integrated requirements for system and organism survival.

At the time, I just wanted to graduate veterinary school and help the animals of the world. I knew and understood organic systems, but I never stopped to think about the necessary business systems that would make my business survive and thrive. The extent of my veterinary school business trained consisted of watching a VHS videotape in the basement of the Large Animal Clinic at the University of Illinois. This, in combination with four years of academic force-feeding, supposedly prepared me to be my own boss.

After graduation, internship, residency, or whatever path you took, if you entered the world of veterinary practice, you found yourself in a completely different environment from the cloistered halls of the university. You entered a world where medicine and management had to co-exist in the living, breathing entity known as real-life veterinary practice. We all graduated from school as technicians, providers of care, with only the foggiest idea of what it takes to be a manager, let alone an entrepreneur. And, to tell the truth, I was happy being a technician. Can you relate to the following story?

My first dream job turned out to be a scream job from which I ran kicking and screaming within three months of starting. That three-month period taught me more about what not to do than any other experience I had.

How *not* to treat people.

How *not* to treat animals.

How *not* to become successful (in the manner, not the outcome—the owner was very successful in his own way).

It *did* teach me that right out of school, the only thing you do is technical work because that is all that you know and that is all that your boss wants you to know and do. I think I figured out then that I was just going to be somebody's technician for the rest of my life . . . or was I?

After my escape, I spent the next few years gaining some outstanding work experiences that provided me a very strong clinical foundation, while concurrently providing a taste of different management and leadership styles. I was becoming a better and better technician, but I was doing it for someone else.

About two-and-a-half years out of school, I was driving around and watching the rapid construction of homes in South Orange County, California, when it hit me (so strongly I had to pull on to the side of the road): one, I had found an outstanding location for a veterinary practice; and two, I had my entrepreneurial seizure. I had to own a practice! It's not that I didn't enjoy what I was doing; I was just doing it for someone else. I had ideas of how I wanted to do things clinically and from a business standpoint, but it wasn't my business within which to do so.

I needed to go out on my own and just do it. So I did.

You start your business with high hopes and expectations, but no real direction, so it spirals from there. Your job as a technician is to keep the patients from dying. Your job as a manager is to keep the operations from dying. Your job as an owner is to keep the entire business from dying. And you are doing this with no foundational knowledge of what you are doing.

There is a lot more to running a veterinary practice than one observes as a technician in an exam room, surgery suite, or business office. The chaos that is pervasive in a veterinary practice doesn't go away just because you own the business. It just becomes your chaos. The patients don't change, the clients don't change, the bills don't change, the headaches don't change, the staff doesn't change. They just become your patients, clients, bills, headaches, and staff.

My frustration settled in about a year into owning my practice. While attending a huge veterinary conference in Las Vegas, I heard my name called over the casino pager: *Dr. Peter Weinstein, please pick up the nearest white courtesy phone*. As a husband and son, you always worry about that page. As a business owner, you practically panic about that page: did the practice burn down? Did nobody show up to open the business? Are we bankrupt already? Or, as was the case this time, was a client unwilling to see the doctor working that day because it wasn't me? I realized then and there that the practice owned me. As Michael says, I was working for a lunatic, and one who I couldn't avoid because I saw him in the mirror every day. When the light at the end of the tunnel is a train, what do you do?

By year three of ownership, I was completely burned out and burned up. There was no relief in sight, and unlike other jobs, I couldn't just quit this one. As Michael notes, every business is a family business, and although my wife at the time didn't participate directly with the business, the stresses, aggravations, and frustrations I carried home influenced everything—and not in a good way. The practice was sucking the life out of me and, as a result, my home life was sucking too. We went on vacation to get away from it all and in a blinding flash, the obvious hit me: things needed to change.

I returned to my practice determined to find a different way of doing things. But it wasn't easy. All of the resources for veterinary practices pretty much said keep working hard, take good care of the animals and their owners, and the money will come. But it never seemed to come. The animals were cared for. The bills were paid. The staff was paid. And I wondered when I would ever be able to pay myself.

Epiphany

While attending a continuing education forum, one of the speakers mentioned *The E-Myth* by Michael Gerber and suggested it would be a great resource to help any veterinarian owner (or owner wannabe) understand how to run his business. More specifically, how to create systems to run his business, and how that system would allow him to work on the business and not just in the business.

I bought the book and read it once. I digested it a second time. The third time, I drank the Kool-Aid. I was hooked.

Fortunately, Mr. Gerber was also out speaking about the concepts, theories, and facts expounded upon in his book, so I went to hear him speak. Not just once, but many times. I became a Gerber stalker. I spoke to his coaches in the offices and became more and more ingrained in the E-Myth philosophy.

Finally, all of the systems that I had learned about in school and at which I had become very good at examining, diagnosing, and treating, were applied to creating systems in my veterinary practice.

I went to work on my business by creating the systems necessary for my business to run without me. And it started to turn around. Slowly, but surely things got easier, more predictable, less chaotic, and more consistent. The work would get done. I could focus on bigger-picture needs, and I didn't have to run out and pick up toilet paper at lunch.

By engaging my team to help build the systems, processes, and checklists, we were able to develop an operations manual that helped old and new employees alike deliver a more engaging experience for our clients. Was it perfect? No, but it was getting there.

The experience of working on the business and creating operations, management, money, planning, and other systems allowed for consistent growth, consistent profits, and eventually a business that became a part of a larger enterprise (a corporate consolidator).

Rut vs. Grave

Do you know what the difference is between a rut and a grave? The depth.

In my opinion, there is no healthcare provider (MD, DDS, DO, DC) whose business is as complex, with so many moving parts and people, as a veterinary office. We provide medical and surgical care in one facility that the other health care providers outsource to multiple venues. Radiology, laboratory work, surgery, well-care are all under one roof and housed concurrently with bathing, grooming, and supplies. What other health care profession has as many different services all delivered at the same time?

Is there any other health care profession that has as high a staff-to-doctor ratio as most veterinary practices? Veterinarians are surrounded by receptionists (client service representatives), animal health technicians (licensed), unlicensed assistants, animal caretakers (kennel help), managers, and groomers, all of whom are challenged to provide a world-class experience to the client and the patient. And, in most cases, there is *no* system in place. Because the only thing that is consistent about a veterinary practice is its inconsistency!

Veterinarians are a perfect profession in which to dream of more control and less chaos; of appointment books that are organized; of surgical cases that move in and out smoothly; of appointments that flow with predictable ease; of staff who come to work empowered, engaged, empathetic, and excited about their careers. There is no profession that could benefit more from getting organized, processed, check-listed, reciped, and systematized than veterinary medicine.

Have you ever thought about who your practice impacts? And that how you feel about your practice impacts those around you? And how a bad day is carried home to impact your family? And how there are more bad days than good days? You can't extricate you from your business since you spend more of your waking hours at work than at play.

So, doesn't it make sense to work on your business to allow you to have more good days than bad? More home days than work? More future than past?

Start to shift your focal point from the here-and-now to the there-and-then. Where do you want your practice to be down the road so it will provide you and your family, your staff and your patients everything that they need or want?

It is time to get out of your rut. I outline the first steps in this book. In the next chapter, Michael starts you down your path to systematizing your success by addressing a topic that makes many of you very uncomfortable: money. Let's see what Michael can teach you about money. ✤

CHAPTER

3

On The Subject of Money

Michael E. Gerber

There are three faithful friends: an old wife, an old dog, and ready money.
—Benjamin Franklin

Had Steve and Peggy first considered the subject of *money* as we will here, their lives could have been radically different.

Money is on the tip of every veterinarian's tongue, on the edge (or at the very center) of every veterinarian's thoughts, intruding on every part of a veterinarian's life.

With money consuming so much energy, why do so few veterinarians handle it well? Why was Steve, like so many veterinarians, willing to entrust his financial affairs to a relative stranger? Why is money scarce for most veterinarians? Why is there less money than expected? And yet the demand for money is always greater than anticipated.

What is it about money that is so elusive, so complicated, so difficult to control? Why is it that every veterinarian I've ever met hates to deal with the subject of money? Why are they almost always too late in facing money problems? And why are they constantly obsessed with the desire for more of it?

Money—you can't live with it and you can't live without it. But you'd better understand it and get your people to understand it. Because until you do, money problems will eat your practice for lunch.

You don't need an accountant or financial planner to do this. You simply need to prod your people to relate to money very personally. From the veterinary technician to the office manager, they all should understand the financial impact of what they do every day in relationship to the profit and loss of the practice.

And so you must teach your people to think like owners, not like technicians or office managers. You must teach them to operate like personal profit centers, with a sense of how their work fits in with the practice as a whole.

You must involve everyone in the practice with the topic of money—how it works, where it goes, how much is left, and how much everybody gets at the end of the day. You also must teach them about the four kinds of money created by the practice.

The Four Kinds of Money

In the context of owning, operating, developing, and exiting from a veterinary practice, money can be split into four distinct but highly integrated categories:

- Income
- Profit
- Flow
- Equity

Failure to distinguish how the four kinds of money play out in your practice is a surefire recipe for disaster.

Important Note: Do not talk to your accountants or bookkeepers about what follows; it will only confuse them and you. The information comes from the real-life experiences of thousands of small-business owners, veterinarians included, most of whom were hopelessly confused about money when I met them. Once they understood and accepted the following principles, they developed a clarity about money that could only be called enlightened.

The First Kind of Money: Income

Income is the money veterinarians are paid by their practice for doing their job in the practice. It's what they get paid for going to work every day.

Clearly, if veterinarians didn't do their job, others would have to, and *they* would be paid the money the practice currently pays those veterinarians. Income, then, has nothing to do with *ownership*. Income is solely the province of *employee-ship*.

That's why to the veterinarian-as-*employee*, income is the most important form money can take. To the veterinarian-as-*owner*, however, it is the least important form money can take.

Most important; least important. Do you see the conflict? The conflict between the veterinarian-as-employee and the veterinarian-as-owner?

We'll deal with this conflict later. For now, just know that it is potentially the most paralyzing conflict in a veterinarian's life.

Failing to resolve this conflict will cripple you. Resolving it will set you free.

The Second Kind of Money: Profit

Profit is what's left over after a veterinary practice has done its job effectively and efficiently. If there is no profit, the practice is doing something wrong.

However, just because the practice shows a profit does not mean it is necessarily doing all the right things in the right way. Instead, it just means that something was done right during or preceding the period in which the profit was earned.

The important issue here is whether the profit was intentional or accidental. If it happened by accident (which most profit does), don't take credit for it. You'll live to regret your impertinence.

If it happened intentionally, take all the credit you want. You've earned it. Because profit created intentionally, rather than by accident, is replicable—again and again. And your practice's ability to repeat its performance is the most critical ability it can have.

As you'll soon see, the value of money is a function of your practice's ability to produce it in predictable amounts at an above-average return on investment.

Profit can be understood only in the context of your practice's purpose, as opposed to your purpose as a veterinarian. Profit, then, fuels the forward motion of the practice that produces it. This is accomplished in four ways:

- Profit is *investment capital* that feeds and supports growth.
- Profit is *bonus capital* that rewards people for exceptional work.
- Profit is *operating capital* that shores up money shortfalls.
- Profit is *return-on-investment capital* that rewards you, the veterinarian-owner, for taking risks.

Without profit, a veterinary practice cannot subsist, much less grow. Profit is the fuel of progress.

If a practice misuses or abuses profit, however, the penalty is much like having no profit at all. Imagine the plight of a veterinarian who has way too much return-on-investment capital and not enough investment capital, bonus capital, and operating capital. Can you see the imbalance this creates?

The Third Kind of Money: Flow

Flow is what money *does* veterinary practice, as opposed to what money *is*. Whether the practice is large or small, money tends to move erratically through it, much like a pinball. One minute it's there; the next minute it's not.

Flow can be even more critical to a practice's survival than profit, because a practice can produce a profit and still be short of money. Has this ever happened to you? It's called profit on paper rather than in fact.

No matter how large your practice, if the money isn't there when it's needed, you're threatened—regardless of how much profit you've made. You can borrow it, of course. But money acquired in dire circumstances is almost always the most expensive kind of money you can get.

Knowing where the money is and where it will be when you need it is a critically important task of both the veterinarian-as-employee and the veterinarian-as-owner.

Rules of Flow

You will learn no more important lesson than the huge impact flow can have on the health and survival of your veterinary practice, let alone your business or enterprise. The following two rules will help you understand why this subject is so critical.

1. **The First Rule of Flow states that your income statement is static, while the flow is dynamic.** Your income statement is a snapshot, while the flow is a moving picture. So, while your income statement is an excellent tool for analyzing your practice *after* the fact, it's a poor tool for managing it in the heat of the moment.

Your income statement tells you (1) how much money you're spending and where, and (2) how much money you're receiving and from where.

Flow gives you the same information as the income statement, plus it tells you *when* you're spending and receiving money. In other words, flow is an income statement moving through time. And that is the key to understanding flow. It is about management in real time. How much is coming in? How much is going out? You'd like to know this daily, or even by the hour if possible. Never by the week or month.

You must be able to forecast flow. You must have a flow plan that helps you gain a clear vision of the money that's out there next month and the month after that. You must also pinpoint what your needs will be in the future.

Ultimately, however, when it comes to flow, the action is always in the moment. It's about *now*. The minute you start to meander away from the present, you'll miss the boat.

Unfortunately, few veterinarians pay any attention to flow until it dries up completely and slow pay becomes no pay. They are oblivious to this kind of detail until business drops off dramatically. That gets a veterinarian's attention because the expenses keep on coming.

When it comes to flow, most veterinarians are flying by the proverbial seat of their pants. No matter how many people you hire to take care of your money, until you change the way you think about it, you will always be out of luck. No one can do this for you.

Managing flow takes attention to detail. But when flow is managed, your life takes on an incredible sheen. You're swimming with the current, not against it. You're in charge!

2. **The Second Rule of Flow states that money seldom moves as you expect it to.** But you do have the power to change that, provided you understand the two primary sources of money as it comes in and goes out of your veterinary practice.

The truth is, the more control you have over the source of money, the more control you have over its flow. The sources of money are both inside and outside your practice.

Money comes from outside your practice in the form of service fees, and receivables.

Money comes from inside your practice in the form of payables, taxes, and payroll. These are the costs associated with attracting patients, delivering your services, operations, and so forth.

Few veterinarians see the money going out of their practice as a source of money, but it is.

When considering how to spend money in your practice, you can save—and therefore make—money in three ways:

- Do it more effectively.
- Do it more efficiently.
- Stop doing it altogether.

By identifying the money sources inside and outside your practice, and then applying these methods, you will be immeasurably better at controlling the flow in your practice.

But what are these sources? They include how you

- manage your services;
- buy supplies and equipment;
- compensate your people;
- plan people's use of time;
- determine the direct cost of your services;
- increase the number of patients seen;
- manage your work;
- collect reimbursements and receivables; and
- countless more.

In fact, every task performed in your practice (and ones you haven't yet learned how to perform) can be done more efficiently and effectively, dramatically reducing the cost of doing business. In the process, you will create more income, produce more profit, and balance the flow.

The Fourth Kind of Money: Equity

Sadly, few veterinarians fully appreciate the value of equity in their veterinary practice. Yet equity is the second most valuable asset any veterinarian will ever possess. (The first most valuable asset is, of course, your life. More on that later.)

Equity is the financial value placed on your veterinary practice by a prospective buyer.

Thus, your *practice* is your most important product, not your services. Because your practice has the power to set you free. That's right. Once you sell your practice—providing you get what you want for it—you're free!

Of course, to enhance your equity, to increase your practice's value, you have to build it right. You have to build a practice that works. A practice that can become a true business and a business that can become a true enterprise. A practice/business/enterprise that can produce income, profit, flow, and equity better than any other veterinarian's practice can.

To accomplish that, your practice must be designed so that it can do what it does systematically and predictably, every single time.

The Story of McDonald's

Let me tell you the most unlikely story anyone has ever told you about the successful building of a veterinary practice, business, and enterprise. Let me tell you the story of Ray Kroc.

You might be thinking, "What on earth does a hamburger stand have to do with my practice? I'm not in the hamburger business; I'm a veterinarian."

Yes, you are. But by practicing veterinary medicine as you have been taught, you've abandoned any chance to expand your reach, help more patients, or improve your services the way they must be improved if the veterinary business—and your life—is going to be transformed.

In Ray Kroc's story lies the answer.

Kroc called his first McDonald's restaurant "a little money machine." That's why thousands of franchises bought it. And the reason it worked? Kroc demanded consistency, so that a hamburger in Philadelphia would be an advertisement for one in Peoria. In fact, no matter where you bought a McDonald's hamburger in the 1950s, the meat patty was guaranteed to weigh exactly 1.6 ounces, with a diameter of 3 ⅝ inches. It was in the McDonald's handbook.

Did Kroc succeed? You know he did! And so can you, once you understand his methods. Consider just one part of his story.

In 1954, Kroc made his living selling the five-spindle Multimixer milkshake machine. He heard about a hamburger stand in San Bernardino, California, that had eight of his machines in operation, meaning it could make forty shakes simultaneously. This he had to see.

Kroc flew from Chicago to Los Angeles, then drove 60 miles to San Bernardino. As he sat in his car outside Mac and Dick McDonald's restaurant, he watched as lunch customers lined up for bags of hamburgers.

In a revealing moment, Kroc approached a strawberry blonde in a yellow convertible. As he later described it, "It was not her sex appeal but the obvious relish with which she devoured the hamburger that made my pulse begin to hammer with excitement."

Passion.

In fact, it was the French fry that truly captured his heart. Before the 1950s, it was almost impossible to buy fries of consistent quality. Kroc changed all that. "The French fry," he once wrote, "would become almost sacrosanct for me, its preparation a ritual to be followed religiously."

Passion and preparation.

The potatoes had to be just so—top-quality Idaho russets, 8 ounces apiece, deep-fried to a golden brown, and salted with a shaker that, as Kroc put it, kept going "like a Salvation Army girl's tambourine."

As Kroc soon learned, potatoes too high in water content—even top-quality Idaho russets varied greatly in water content—will come out soggy when fried. And so Kroc sent out teams of workers, armed with hydrometers, to make sure all his suppliers were producing potatoes in the optimal solids range of 20 percent to 23 percent.

Preparation and passion. Passion and preparation. Look those words up in the dictionary and you'll see Kroc's picture. Can you envision your picture there?

Do you understand what Kroc did? Do you see why he was able to sell thousands of franchises? Kroc knew the true value of equity, and, unlike Steve from our story, Kroc went to work *on* his business rather than *in* his business. He knew the hamburger wasn't his product—McDonald's was!

So what does *your* dental practice need to do to become a little money machine? What is the passion that will drive you to build a practice that works—a turnkey system like Ray Kroc's?

Equity and the Turnkey System

What's a turnkey system? And why is it so valuable to you? To better understand it, let's look at another example of a turnkey system that worked to perfection: the recordings of Frank Sinatra.

Frank Sinatra's records were to him as McDonald's restaurants were to Ray Kroc. They were part of a turnkey system that allowed Sinatra to sing to millions of people without having to be there himself.

Sinatra's recordings were a dependable turnkey system that worked predictably, systematically, automatically, and effortlessly to produce the same results every single time—no matter where they were played, and no matter who was listening.

Regardless of where Frank Sinatra was, his records just kept on producing income, profit, flow, and equity, over and over. . .and still do! Sinatra needed only to produce the prototype recording, and the system did the rest.

Kroc's McDonald's is another prototypical turnkey solution, addressing everything McDonald's needs to do in a basic, systematic way so that anyone properly trained by McDonald's can successfully reproduce the same results.

And this is where you'll realize your equity opportunity: in the way your practice does business, in the way your practice systematically does what you intend it to do, and in the development of your turnkey system—a system that works even in the hands of ordinary people (and veterinarians less experienced than you) to produce extraordinary results.

Remember:

- If you want to build vast equity in your practice, then go to work on your practice, building it into a business that works every single time.
- Go to work *on* your practice to build a totally integrated turnkey system that delivers exactly what you promised every single time.
- Go to work *on* your practice to package it and make it stand out from the veterinary practices you see everywhere else.

Here is the most important idea you will ever hear about your practice and what it can potentially provide for you:

The value of your equity is directly proportional to how well your practice works. And how well your practice works is directly proportional to the effectiveness of the systems you have put into place upon which the operation of your practice depends.

Whether money takes the form of income, profit, flow, or equity, the amount of it—and how much of it stays with you—invariably boils down to this. Money, happiness, life—it all depends on how well your practice works. Not on your people, not on you, but on the system.

Your practice holds the secret to more money. Are you ready to learn how to find it?

Earlier in this chapter, I alerted you to the inevitable conflict between the veterinarian-as-employee and the veterinarian-as-owner. It's a battle between the part of you working in the practice and the part of you working on the practice. Between the part of you working for income and the part of you working for equity.

Here's how to resolve this conflict:

- Be honest with yourself about whether you're filling *employee* shoes or *owner* shoes.
- As your practice's key employee, determine the most effective way to do the job you're doing, *and then document that job.*

- Once you've documented the job, create a strategy for replacing yourself with someone else (another veterinarian) who will then use your documented system exactly as you do.
- Have your new employees manage the newly delegated system. Improve the system by quantifying its effectiveness over time.
- Repeat this process throughout your practice wherever you catch yourself acting as employee rather than *owner*.
- Learn to distinguish between ownership work and employeeship work every step of the way.

Master these methods, understand the difference between the four kinds of money, develop an interest in how money works in your practice . . . and then watch it flow in with the speed and efficiency of a perfectly pounded hammer.

Now let's take another step in our strategic thinking process. Let's look at the subject of *planning*. But first, let's see what Peter has to say about money. ✤

CHAPTER

4

Money Makes the World Go Round

Peter Weinstein, DVM, MBA

When it comes to money, you can't win. If you focus on making it, you're materialistic. If you try to but don't make any, you're a loser. If you make a lot and keep it, you're a miser. If you make it and spend it, you're a spendthrift. If you don't care about making it, you're unambitious. If you make a lot and still have it when you die, you're a fool—for trying to take it with you. The only way to really win with money is to hold it loosely—and be generous with it to accomplish things of value.

—John C. Maxwell, *Motivated to Succeed*

As we begin our conversation about money we venture into uncomfortable territory—yet it's a vitally important conversation to have, so let's risk discomfort momentarily as we explore the challenges of making money as an entrepreneurial veterinarian.

As a young kennel kid in the '70s, I was in awe of all of the people waiting to see Drs. Kronfeld and Mann. The amount of cash transactions back then was awe-inspiring. The upscale cars that they drove were motivational. Here was a gig where I could do something great, fix animals, and be financially successful. Sign me up!

But as an entrepreneur with my own practice, I soon realized the money part of the equation was the most challenging. Being socially conscious, I focused on doing good for the animals and society, frequently to my own financial detriment. Making money was less important than the vomiting puppy owned by an eleven year old, or the Shih Tzu with glaucoma that was the last memory of the client's late husband. At some point, veterinary medicine decided that being socially focused and financially focused were mutually exclusive. Why? It doesn't make financial sense.

We veterinarians want to be loved, and if money was the barrier to being loved, then so be it—we will sacrifice income to be loved.

Frank Sovinsky, the E-Myth Chiropractor, addressed this beautifully for the chiropractic profession and it is worth extrapolating to the veterinary profession:

"As healthcare providers, our altruistic nature can conflict with the utilitarian reality of owning a business. Making a profit is *not* incompatible with your social obligation. In fact, it is essential."

After my entrepreneurial seizure—like Wolfman at midnight—my life changed. I recognized that to pay myself, pay off loans, and pay the bills, I have to rethink money. It didn't mean that I totally understood it at first; I just knew that money makes all the difference.

Money in Practice

In a veterinary practice, there are two ways an employed veterinarian associate can make money: a salary and bonuses. So to get "rich", you see more clients, charge more per client, and hop onto every income-generating opportunity you can.

The veterinarian owner, on the other hand, has four ways to make money: salary, management fees (if he wears that hat, too), rent or mortgage, and return on investment (ROI, profit, net, or equity). However, without understanding these different types of money, the owner sees it all as one lump sum without understanding where it came from and how to use it. So the owner DVM continues to act as an employee, focusing strictly on production.

On the other hand, the veterinary entrepreneur working on his business seeks to optimize those four sources of money. Systems are built for money creation and expense control. Equity is created to ensure the long-term value of money. Short-term values pay the bills; long-term values pay for college education and retirement. Equity is your exit strategy. Investment is your retirement strategy.

I have seen this scenario all too often: Income comes in. Bills get paid. Salaries get paid. What's left over goes to the owner. This may leave a little bit behind for the slow week, month, year, or decade. Rather than investing back into the business, the business is strictly a source for income. The gratification is immediate, but the long-term vision is absent.

In speaking with financial planners and bankers and hospital brokers, more important than an individual salary taken by the owner is the profitability and cash flow of the practice. As an owner looks down the road, the deeper one's individual pockets, the shallower equity (on paper) may be for the business. In other words, eating well now may lead to starving later—later being retirement. Of course, this sow-reap-consume mentality has left many practice owners practicing well into their seventies, and even eighties, because their field laid barren over the years.

The minute I figured out that money was not evil and that quality medicine and quality business could exist hand-in-hand, I discovered that working *on* the business was more fun than working *in* the business.

The Money System

Practically speaking, though, *how* do you systematize money? In short: reprogramming first how you see money and your business, and second your actual business systems.

Begin by realizing that everything you do to systematize your practice impacts the money discussion. Every source of income—client service; exam room discussions; collection of fees; creation of health care plans; fee schedule—impacts the top line. The more consistent and predictable you make everything you do, the more income you'll have.

Every expense— shopping for best prices; hiring and firing; equipment purchases; repairs and maintenance; adding an associate—can be systematized to minimize money flowing out of your practice. If you maximize your income while minimizing your expenses, you optimize profitability. And just like that, you elevate your equity in the business.

Over the last few years, it has become more and more apparent that the sale of your business will not provide sufficient return to allow you to exit comfortably and simply retire. With practice values based upon cash flow, it is more and more important to build a practice that works by itself and the profitability of which allows for not only long-term returns, but also short-term returns of investable income. By neglecting to systematize your business, and simply putting your head down and working, working, working, you don't build up equity; you build up callouses.

It didn't take long for me to learn to focus farther down the road and create a profitable entity that was valuable to a buyer. The proper systems in place and a healthy profit on the books made for an attractive purchase. And who wants to look a gift horse in the mouth? Money talked and I walked.

A Budget

So where do you start? With a budget. A budget itself is a system, and the process of creating one should be a fundamental part of your business. Add to the budget a series of readily determined key performance indicators with associated benchmarks, and you can easily see where you are daily, weekly, monthly, and annually. All of these numbers are collected in a predictable fashion, reproduced in repeatable tabular form, reviewed in a systematic fashion, and discussed with hospital leadership with the ultimate goal of tweaking the systems to continually improve the numbers.

If you don't measure it, you can't manage it. The typical veterinary practice handles its books like this: Balance them at the end of the day; put the money into a safe until it is deposited the next day; place the end-of-day reports in a special drawer in the owner's desk. Every week or two, the owner, manager, or bookkeeper pays the bills. That person creates a financial report using a computer program like QuickBooks and puts it into that same special drawer.

The daily financial and monthly financial reports sit in that special drawer until one day you go to pay the bills and there's not enough money in the bank. Finally, that great Egyptian river, De Nile (denial), sets in. You are so busy that you don't think you need to look at the reports. Because if you are busy, you must be making money, right? *Wrong*.

On the other hand, a well-organized and E-Myth'd practice has a daily snapshot, a weekly profile, a monthly overview, and an annual assessment of certain key parameters that, similar to temperature, pulse, and respiration, can tell you the overall health of your patient—the practice. From these reports, you can determine how to treat the patient to make it better, more profitable, and thus increase the health of your business. Or you can continue to fill your drawers.

I never missed reviewing the daily totals, weekly totals, and monthly totals. We had a series of numbers we tracked that helped us gauge success and prosperity. Month-to-month and year-to-year comparisons gave me information to help steer the ship, modify a system, or change our marketing plan. By having guidelines and responding to them, I created a fluid business that was responsive, not reactive to change, and less susceptible to economic challenges. A budget and benchmarks were tools that I used to keep on the straight-and-narrow.

Fees

As healthcare professionals, veterinarians are readily lumped into the category of doctors, dentists, optometrists, and chiropractors by the plethora of money advisors out there. But we veterinarians really are different.

The veterinary profession does not work under the same challenges as do other health care fields. Insurance companies do not dictate what we charge; veterinary fee schedules and service schedules are determined by the practice ownership. High fee schedules are usually associated with practices that focus on client service, more time with the patients, and higher-quality medicine. On the other hand, lower fee schedules are usually based upon more transactions at a lower fee and can be just as profitable as fewer transactions at a higher fee. And then there are those practice models that are Chimeras from above and try to be everything to everybody while, in reality, being nothing to anybody.

Veterinary fees are not a science in most practices. In fact, in 1989, when I opened my first practice, the going rate for an office visit in Southern California was 100 times the cost of a postage stamp. Since a postage stamp cost $0.25, a typical office call was $25. I set mine at $27 because I wanted to send the message that we were high-value and high-quality care.

Once the office call fee is set, the rest is pretty logical: call around and see what everybody else is charging, or charge more for what you don't like to do and what clients don't want to do, and keep the commodities competitive. Bottom line: There is no rhyme or reason to most veterinary fee schedules, and they rarely reflect the complexity of the procedure, nor do they support the financial needs of the practice.

Making Money Work for You

As veterinarians, we tend to behave schizophrenically. Our personalities range from the generous veterinarian providing affordable healthcare to our patients and their owners, to the greedy, money-hungry business owners who pocket all the profits, never share with the staff, and gouge clients through fees.

Learning how to differentiate the veterinarian owner hat, from the veterinarian doctor or technician hat, from the veterinarian manager hat will go a long way to understanding *how* to react to money and *what* to do with it.

Veterinarian doctors would give their services away for free if it allowed them to provide the needed patient care. They enjoy being a healthcare provider so much that the money is secondary. . .maybe even tertiary.

The veterinarian manager realizes that the money allows the practice to remain open, pay the staff, and deliver services.

The veterinarian owner recognizes that the money pays college tuitions, allows for vacations, and—if they really get it—sets him up for a comfortable retirement where work is an option, *not* a necessity.

At the end of the day, the week, the month, the year, it is what you do with the money that flows to you that determines your short- and long-term success.

It is not the salary that determines your future; it is what you do with it.

It is not the daily receipts that determine your future; it is what you do with them.

It is not your practice that determines your retirement; it is how your practice operates.

Veterinarians right now are working longer days and more years than ever before. Of course, it could be because they love their jobs. Unfortunately, you must also love your boss—you look at him or her every day. More likely, though, they are putting in more hours because they can't afford to *not* work. And why must they continue to toil? No vision, no strategy, no plans!

Speaking of plans, let's listen to Michael's advice on planning in the next chapter.

SIDE NOTE—The Veterinary Student

Currently, the average veterinary student graduates from veterinary school with approximately $170,000 in debt and an average starting salary for a small-animal associate of $70,000. This debt combined with undergraduate and professional school needs to be looked as an investment in a valuable commodity. (Of course, if the debt grew because of splurging for everything that caught your eye, you should come to a Michael Gerber meeting to be reprogrammed about money management.)

It is important to understand that student debt is not a barrier to entrepreneurship. In fact, the best way to retire debt is to recognize that as an owner running a successful systematized business, you will be paid more handsomely than a lifetime of being an associate.

The banks do not hold student debt against you when it comes to ownership. The most important pieces of information that the banks look at are cash flow and profitability. (Other factors include your credit rating and other personal variables that indicate your ability to run a business. In these cases, your past could determine your future.) And, as noted above, more equity comes from a well-run business.

If you are a veterinary student reading this, or an associate thinking of becoming an owner, action item number one should be to create a personal budget and learn how to balance your income and expenses. Intelligently invest money coming in (wages, loans, family) in the necessities of life (food, education, housing) and don't squander it on lavish, selfish, entitled needs. The banks may look at the Porsche and think, *Student loans go to a Porsche? Where will income from the practice go? To a Cessna?* ✤

CHAPTER

5

On the Subject of Planning

Michael E. Gerber

Luck is good planning, carefully executed.

—Anonymous

Another obvious oversight revealed in Steve and Peggy's story was the absence of true planning.

Every veterinarian starting his or her own practice must have a plan. You should never begin to see patients without a plan in place. But, like Steve, most veterinarians do exactly that.

A veterinarian lacking a vision is simply someone who goes to work every day. Someone who is just doing it, doing it, doing it. Busy, busy, busy. Maybe making money, maybe not. Maybe getting something out of life, maybe not. Taking chances without really taking control.

The plan tells anyone who needs to know *how we do things here*. The plan defines the objective and the process by which you will attain it. The plan encourages you to organize tasks into functions, and then helps people grasp the logic of each of those functions. This, in turn, permits you to bring new employees up to speed quickly.

There are numerous books and seminars on the subject of practice management, but they focus on making you a better veterinarian. I want to teach you something else that you've never been taught before: how to be a manager. It has nothing to do with conventional practice management and everything to do with thinking like an entrepreneur.

The Planning Triangle

As we discussed in the Preface, every veterinary sole proprietorship is a practice, every veterinary business is a practice, and every veterinary enterprise is a practice. Yet the difference between the three is extraordinary. Although all three may offer veterinary services, how they do what they do is completely different.

The trouble with most practices owned by veterinarians is that they are dependent on the veterinarian. That's because they're a sole proprietorship—the smallest, most limited form a practice can take. Sole proprietorships are formed around the technician, whether veterinarian or roofer.

You may choose in the beginning to form a practice, but you should understand its limitations. The practice called a *sole proprietorship* depends on the owner—that is, the veterinarian. The practice called a business depends on other people, plus a system by which that business does what it does. Once your practice becomes a business, you can replicate it, turning it into an enterprise.

Consider the example of Sea Veterinary Clinic. The patients don't come in asking for Douglas Sea, although he is one of the top veterinarians around. After all, he can only handle so many patients a day and be in only one location at a time.

Yet he wants to offer his high-quality services to more people in the community. If he has reliable systems in place—systems that any qualified staff member can learn to use—he has created a business and it can be replicated. Douglas can then go on to offer his services—which demand his guidance, not his presence—in a multitude of different settings. He can open dozens of veterinary practices, none of which need Douglas Sea himself, except in the role of entrepreneur.

Is your veterinary practice going to be a sole proprietorship, a business, or an enterprise? Planning is crucial to answering this all-important question. Whatever you choose to do must be communicated by your plan, which are really three interrelated plans in one. We call it the Planning Triangle, and it looks like this:

- The Business Plan;
- The Practice Plan;
- The Completion Plan.

The three plans form a triangle, with the business plan at the base, the practice plan in the center, and the completion plan at the apex.

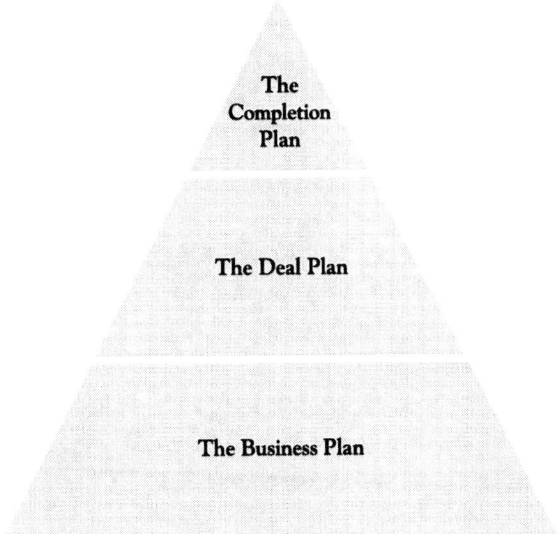

The business plan determines *who* you are (the business); the practice plan determines *what* you do (the specific focus of your veterinary practice); and the completion plan determines *how* you do it (the fulfillment process).

By looking at the Planning Triangle, we see that the three critical plans are interconnected. The connection between them is established by asking the following questions:

1. Who are we?
2. What do we do?
3. How do we do it?

Who are we? is purely a strategic question.

What do we do? is both a strategic and a tactical question.

How do we do it? is both a strategic and a tactical question.

Strategic questions shape the vision and destiny of your business, of which your practice is only one essential component. Tactical questions turn that vision into reality. Thus, strategic questions provide the foundation for tactical questions, just as the base provides the foundation for the middle and apex of your Planning Triangle.

First ask: What do we do, and how do we do it *strategically?*

And then: What do we do, and how do we do it *practically?*

Let's look at how the three plans will help you develop your practice.

The Business Plan

Your business plan will determine what you choose to do in your veterinary practice and the way you choose to do it. Without a business plan, your practice can do little more than survive. And even that will take more than a little luck.

Without a business plan, you're treading water in a deep pool with no shore in sight. You're working against the natural flow.

Your business plan must clearly describe

- the business you are creating;
- the purpose it will serve;
- the vision it will pursue;
- the process through which you will turn that vision into a reality; and
- the way money will be used to realize your vision.

Build your business plan with *business* language, not *practice* language (the veterinarian's language). Make sure the plan focuses on matters of interest to your lenders and shareholders rather than just your technicians. It should rely on demographics and psychographics to tell you who buys and why; it should also include projections for return on investment and return on equity. Use it to detail both the market and the strategy through which you intend to become a leader in that market, not as a veterinarian but as a business enterprise.

The business plan, though absolutely essential, is only one of three critical plans every veterinarian needs to create and implement. Now let's take a look at the practice plan.

The Practice Plan

The practice plan includes everything a veterinarian needs to know, have, and do in order to deliver his or her promise to a patient on time, every time.

Every task should prompt you to ask three questions:

1. What do I need to know?
2. What do I need to have?
3. What do I need to do?

What Do I Need to *Know?*

What information do I need to satisfy my promise on time, every time, exactly as promised? In order to recognize what you need to know, you must understand the expectations of others, including your patients, your associates, and other employees. Are you clear on those expectations? Don't make the mistake of assuming you know. Instead, create a need-to-know checklist to make sure you ask all the necessary questions.

A need-to-know checklist might look like this:

- What are the expectations of my patients?
- What are the expectations of my administrators?
- What are the expectations of my associate veterinarians?
- What are the expectations of my staff?

What Do I Need to *Have?*

This question raises the issue of resources—namely, money, people, and time. If you don't have enough money to finance operations, how can you fulfill those expectations without creating cash-flow problems? If you don't have enough trained people, what happens then? And if you don't have enough time to manage your practice, what happens when you can't be in two places at once?

Don't assume that you can get what you need when you need it. Most often, you can't. And even if you can get what you need at the last minute, you'll pay dearly for it.

What Do I Need to *Do?*

The focus here is on actions to be started and finished. What do I need to do to fulfill the expectations of this patient on time, every time, exactly as promised? For example, what exactly are the steps to perform when approached by a distressed pet owner who seeks emergency help?

Your patients fall into distinct categories, and those categories make up your business. The best veterinary practices will invariably focus on fewer and fewer categories as they discover the importance of doing one thing better than anyone else.

Answering the question *What do I need to do?* demands a series of action plans, including

- the objective to be achieved;
- the standards by which you will know that the objective has been achieved;
- the benchmarks you need to reach in order for the objective to be achieved;
- the function/person accountable for the completion of the benchmarks;
- the budget for the completion of each benchmark; and
- the time by which each benchmark must be completed.

Your action plans should become the foundation for the completion plan. And the reason you need completion plan is to ensure that everything you do is not only realistic but can also be managed.

The Completion Plan

If the practice plan gives you results and provides you with standards, the completion plan tells you everything you need to know about every benchmark in the deal plan—that is, how you're going to fulfill patient expectations on time, every time, as promised. In other words, how you're going to arrange a referral to another veterinarian, conduct routine procedures, or educate a pet owner about treatment options.

The completion plan is essentially the operations manual, providing information about the details of doing tactical work. It is a guide to tell the people responsible for doing that work exactly how to do it.

Every completion plan becomes a part of the knowledge base of your business. No completion plan goes to waste. Every completion plan becomes a kind of textbook that explains to new employees joining your staff how your practice operates in a way that distinguishes it from all other veterinary practices.

To return to an earlier example, the completion plan for making a Big Mac is explicitly described in the McDonald's

Operation Manual, as is every completion plan needed to run a McDonald's business.

The completion plan for a veterinarian might include the step-by-step details of how to check in a patient, run a competent assessment, prescribe an appropriate treatment, explain to the pet owner the options, and then the steps to properly carry out that treatment. They've learned to do it the same way everyone else has learned to do it. But if you are going to stand out as unique in the minds of your patients, employees, and others, you must invent your own way of doing even ordinary things. Most of that value-added perception will come from your communication skills, your listening skills, your innovative skills in transforming an ordinary visit into a great, value-added patient experience.

Perhaps you'll decide that a mandatory part of your treatment procedure with distressed pet owners is to educate them on their various treatment options. If no other veterinarian that your patient has seen has taken the time to explain these options, you'll immediately set yourself apart. You must constantly raise the questions: *How do we do it here? How* should *we do it here?*

The quality of your answers will determine how effectively you distinguish your practice from every other veterinarian's practice.

Benchmarks

You can measure the movement of your practice—from what it is today to what it will be in the future—using business benchmarks. These are the goals you want your business to achieve during its lifetime.

Your benchmarks should include the following:

- Financial benchmarks
- Emotional benchmarks (the impact your practice will have on everyone who comes into contact with it)
- Performance benchmarks

- Patient benchmarks (Who are they? Why do they come to you? What does your practice give them that no one else does?)
- Employee benchmarks (How do you grow people? How do you find people who want to grow? How do you create a school in your practice that will teach your people skills they can't learn anywhere else?)

Your business benchmarks will reflect (1) the position your practice will hold in the minds and hearts of your patients, employees, and investors; and (2) how you intend to make that position a reality through the systems you develop.

Your benchmarks will describe how your management team will take shape and what systems you will need to develop so that your managers, just like McDonald's managers, will be able to produce the results for which they will be held accountable.

Benefits of the Planning Triangle

By implementing the Planning Triangle, you will discover:

- what your practice will look, act, and feel like when it's fully evolved;
- when that's going to happen;
- how much money you will make; and
- much, much more.

These, then, are the primary purposes of the three critical plans: (1) to clarify precisely what needs to be done to get what the veterinarian wants from his or her practice and life, and (2) to define the specific steps by which it will happen.

First *this* must happen, then *that* must happen. One, two, three. By monitoring your progress, step-by-step, you can determine whether you're on the right track.

That's what planning is all about. It's about creating a standard—a yardstick—against which you will be able to measure your performance.

Failing to create such a standard is like throwing a straw into a hurricane. Who knows where that straw will land?

Have you taken the leap? Have you accepted that the words *business* and *practice* are not synonymous? That a sole proprietorship relies on the veterinarian, and a business relies on other people, plus a system?

Because most veterinarians are control freaks, 99 percent of today's veterinary practices are sole proprietorships, not businesses.

The result, as a friend of mine says, is that "veterinarians are spending all day stamping out fires when all around them the forest is ablaze. They're out of touch, and that veterinarian better take control of the practice before someone else does."

Because veterinarians are never taught to think like businesspeople, the veterinary professional is forever at war with the businessperson. This is especially evident in large, multi-location practices, where bureaucrats (businesspeople) often try to control veterinarians (entrepreneurs). They usually end up treating each other as combatants. In fact, the single greatest reason veterinarians become entrepreneurs is to divorce such bureaucrats and to begin to reinvent the veterinary enterprise.

That's you. Now the divorce is over and a new love affair has begun. You're a veterinarian with a plan! Who wouldn't want to do business with such a person?

Now let's take the next step in our strategic odyssey. Let's take a closer look at the subject of management. But before we do, let's find out what Peter has to say about planning. ✤

CHAPTER 6

Do You Know Where You Are Going?

Peter Weinstein, DVM, MBA

Failing to plan is planning to fail.

—John Wooden

I was very proud of what we were going to accomplish in my practice. We had the vision of providing world-class veterinary medical care in a world-class client service environment. Quite the daunting task I had dreamed up. I knew what I wanted to accomplish; I had *no* idea of how to accomplish it.

As I sat in my office either waiting for patients to arrive or hoping that the flow of patients would slow down, I never had a chance to look through the windshield and see where we were headed or how we were going to get there. I knew where *there* was, but hadn't figured out the most direct path. In the old days, you'd go to AAA and get a Triptik® to map your most direct route. Now you go to Google Maps to help you find your fastest course. With no course to follow except what was in my head, all I wanted was to survive each day.

Between appointments and surgeries, I had to order drugs, go to Costco for toilet paper, rearrange the already rearranged staff schedule, post bail (yes, I did that once), review cases, write up charts, make phone calls, ensure the books balanced, and play amateur psychiatrist. And that was just the first hour or two.

There is an arcade game called Whac-a-Mole. If you picture each of those moles that pops up as the issues that arise on a minute-by-minute basis, you spend your day simply whacking moles! Exhausting! And no extra-large stuffed animal for making it through the game.

Who has time to map your course when you are stuck in a sinkhole? As the busywork overtook the bigger picture, I sank into a malaise. As everybody else got paid and I didn't, I began to wonder, what's so great about being your own boss? Three years into it and I wanted out. As Michael notes, I was working for a lunatic and I saw the lunatic every time I looked in the mirror.

We weren't planning for the future; we were planning for the next appointment. We had the tactics working, and we worked on continuing to improve the tactics for success. But we had absolutely no strategy on how we were going to accomplish my Primary Aim, my Dream. Vet School never prepared me for this.

I was the technician with the entrepreneurial seizure just doing it, doing it, doing it. I was burned out with no relief in sight.

I would go to continuing education programs and learn about dental disease, livers, kidneys, hearts, and skin. When I attended business seminars, the practice-management gurus expounded on the tactics to become more successful and the things you needed to do to get there. But there was no foundation for the tactical ideas, just more to do. There was no guide to escape just doing it, except to just do it.

And then I learned about goal setting and strategic planning. I learned about systems and processes and action plans and working on your business, not just in your business. I became an apostle of the teachings of Gerber. I especially enjoyed the story in *The E-Myth* of his visit to a hotel and the experience that he had from arrival to departure, and everywhere in between. I recognized the bathroom cleanup schedule on the back of the door at McDonalds for what it was:

a process within a system. I wanted a bathroom cleanup schedule in my practice. I wanted a practice that was predictable, consistent, and memorable. But how?

I started to think about working on my business. I started to think more strategically about what I needed to do to get closer to my goals. With the vision in mind, what did we need to support the vision? With the people and resources in place, what did we need to do minute-by-minute, hour-by-hour, day-by-day, week-by-week, month-by-month, year-by-year to stay on the most direct path to the Promised Land?

I had been so entrenched at the molecular level that I never had stepped back and looked at the animal (aka, the hospital) as a whole. It was a hole—one that I was falling deeper into. However, when I took the more holistic approach of looking at the business as a business, and not a dog and cat repair shop, I had a *eureka* moment.

Weekends were spent focusing on the future. Identifying the systems. Breaking the systems into their molecular processes. The telephone answering system had a lot of nuances to it. The surgical system had a lot of details. I never really took time away from the practice to think about it all the way through. Retrospectively, it would have been faster if I had.

So how did I get away from being the one the business depended on to:

- see clients
- call clients
- order food and drugs
- repair sinks
- unclog toilets
- conduct meetings
- go the bank
- learn about new equipment
- price shop services
- and the millions of other tedious tasks of the technician?

There was only one way to find the time to be the manager and entrepreneur and remove the omnipresent technician hat: Learn to trust my people and delegate. But before I delegated, I trained, I taught, I documented and monitored. It wasn't abdication, it was delegation. And I taught the ones to whom I had delegated to delegate.

But not before they had done it right, streamlined it, taught it, documented it, and monitored it.

We were slowly but surely building our training tools, our operations manual, and our resources to ensure we did it the same way, every time without fail. And, most importantly, the next person hired could do it the same way each time, every time, without fail.

Life was not looking quite so bleak anymore, and there was more time to think about the bigger picture.

Applying the Planning Triangle: Controlling the Chaos

Start with a vision. Because your vision defines your destiny.

Creating your vision requires you to wear *only* your entrepreneur hat. Leave the others at home, in the safe, locked up. Whether you lock yourself in your practice office (an OK option), lock yourself in your house (a better option), or get away from it all to a quiet, secluded venue (the best option), you need to be focused and clear-minded. Remember, with no vision, you have no vision.

Then, write it down. Think about it further. Elaborate on it. Discuss it. Brainstorm it. And finally share it with everyone and anyone around you. And then ask, *What is it going to take to get to this vision?*

You need a vision to have a target to shoot for. No vision, you're blind. Your GPS is unprogrammed and you are driving around lost.

Your vision sets your direction for the practice when it is mature. Your plan will be based not upon today, but this vision of your mature practice. If your practice is twenty years old, is it mature (not chronologically), or does it still have some growing to do? Work on your practice as if it were still in its infancy. Your vision should explain why you do what you do, your greater purpose, and how your business will attain that greater purpose.

I had the benefit of a young practice when I started to work on the systems. However, young or old, age is not a disease, so you can create your plan for your mature practice at any time. Think about the daily, weekly, monthly, and annual changes, and they will start to occur. Today's practice is not tomorrow's practice, the practice you will eventually sell.

Your practice vision, when shared, is motivational to everyone around you: family, friends, staff, industry, clients. It sends a message that you know what you want and you are determined to get it, and those around you will be there to help you attain it.

A few more points on visioning: vague doesn't work; be specific. Ask yourself questions and answer them. Questions such as:

- Who am I?
- What is it that I/we do?
- Why do I/we do what we do?
- What is the purpose for which my/our business exists?
- Is there a problem out there that we are going to solve?
- How are we going to solve the problem?
- And finally, who's on our staff?

Plot everything on the Planning Triangle where it fits, and drill it down to the molecular level.

As I sat in my practice, worrying about when I would pay myself, I realized that there were way too many practices around me doing the same thing. We performed exams, vaccinations, intestinal parasite exams, de-sexing procedures, and the like. And people couldn't differentiate what we did from how we did it. To borrow from Seth Godin, we had a herd of Holstein cattle all producing milk. I wanted to be the purple cow. I wanted to be different. I wanted systems and consistency to be the differentiator for my clients.

From Vision to Reality

Translating the Business Plan to the Practice Plan requires more planning time away from the practice. Knowing what you want is one thing; delivering on it is another. There are so many moving parts. What is it your clients and patients want and need? What is it that your hospital staff wants and needs? What are the human resources needed to deliver the vision? What equipment and supplies are needed to provide the world-class experience clinically, and from a service standpoint? What amount of money do we need to have to deliver all of this? And even with all of this in place, how am I going to do this consistently, effectively, efficiently, and predictably?

As we moved from the 35,000-foot vision to the 5,000-foot operations overview, we developed expectations for delivery; essentially guidelines by which each staff member would act to ensure our vision. We looked at how we would do things, and ensured it delivered on our primary aim. Driving each step at this level were the timing, money, people who were accountable, and the perfect outcome. Before we could drill down even further, we needed to understand each of these objectives.

So, we worked on the phones, the exam rooms, the kennels, the treatment area, the surgery suite, the laboratory, the radiology area. We set goals such as:

> **Radiology:** *Perfectly positioned, perfectly exposed radiographs to minimize patient and staff radiation exposure. This saved money from a radiograph film and staff time standpoint. One experienced technician and one animal assistant would be the optimal pairing to take radiographs, with the experienced technician being the one ultimately accountable for the outcome. Depending upon the study, an optimal time needed to accomplish the outcome could be determined.* **Note:** *In veterinary medicine, with the unpredictability of our patients, the outcomes are based upon the 80-percent predictable experiences, with the understanding that about 20 percent of the time there are variables that*

are outside our control, such as fractious cats, aggressive dogs, and fragile patients due to age.

Focus on the way it will work perfectly 80 percent of the time. That is a huge first step.

From Reality to Process

So with the perfect radiograph defined and the expectations clear, we faced the next step: How do we get there? That is the system, the recipe, the completion plan, basically the step-by-step, predictable process to complete the task. This is written down in such exquisite detail that anybody can pick it up and do it with little or no training. It is your standard operating procedure. And each of these becomes a part of your Operations Manual. And each of these is a part of your Training Program. And these are all living, breathing organisms since technology changes, so along the way, more efficient ways of doing things are identified.

How did we get to the molecular level? Easy—you ask someone when they do something to write it down, and then try it to see if it works. Then ask somebody else to do it. If it is simple enough, anybody will be able to pick it up and do it. Each process is assessed regularly and updated as needed.

In football parlance, this is your playbook. It doesn't just sit on a shelf or computer—it is reviewed everyday as new people are trained and experienced people find better ways to do things. It says, this is the way we do things at our practice. Wouldn't your staff love to have a predictable way to doing things. The same way, each time, every time? You know they would. And if you don't believe me, just ask them.

Moving from chaos to control comes by knowing where you want to go, mapping out the trip, and then looking at it step by step to ensure there are no slip-ups or trip-ups.

From my experience, veterinarians are procrastinators and micro-managers and are really good about planning to plan, but not so good at actually planning.

Make time to plan your future. Focus through the windshield on the final product.

Please take the time away from the practice with your leadership team to set up the plans needed. Using your vision as the foundation, everybody needs to take their technician hat off and create the systems needed to attain said vision. In the old way of thinking, your practice managed the people. In the next section, Michael talks about management as managing the systems. What a novel concept! ✦

CHAPTER

7

On the Subject of Management

Michael E. Gerber

Good management consists of showing average people how to do the work of superior people.

—John D. Rockefeller

Every veterinarian, including Steve Walsh from our story, eventually faces the issues of management. Most face it badly.

Why do so many veterinarians suffer from a kind of paralysis when it comes to dealing with management? Why are so few able to get their veterinary practice to work the way they want it to and to run it on time? Why are their managers (if they have any) seemingly so inept?

There are two main problems. First, the veterinarian usually abdicates accountability for management by hiring an office manager. Thus, the veterinarian is working hand in glove with someone who is supposed to do the managing. But the veterinarian is unmanageable himself!

The veterinarian doesn't think like a manager because he doesn't think he is a manager. He's a veterinarian! He rules the roost. And so he gets the office manager to take care of stuff like scheduling appointments, keeping his calendar, collecting receivables, hiring and firing, and much more.

Second, no matter who does the managing, they usually have a completely dysfunctional idea of what it means to manage. They're trying to manage people, contrary to what is needed.

We often hear that a good manager must be a "people person": someone who loves to nourish, figure out, support, care for, teach, baby, monitor, mentor, direct, track, motivate, and—if all else fails—threaten or beat up her people.

Don't believe it. Management has far less to do with people than you've been led to believe.

In fact, despite the claims of every management book written by management gurus (who have seldom managed anything), no one—with the exception of a few bloodthirsty tyrants—has ever learned how to manage people.

And the reason is simple: *People are almost impossible to manage.*

Yes, it's true. People are unmanageable. They're inconsistent, unpredictable, unchangeable, unrepentant, irrepressible, and generally impossible.

Doesn't knowing this make you feel better? Now you understand why you've had all those problems! Do you feel the relief, the heavy stone lifted from your chest?

The time has come to fully understand what management is really all about. Rather than managing *people*, management is really all about managing a *process*, a step-by-step way of doing things, which, combined with other processes, becomes a system. For example:

- The process for on-time scheduling
- The process for answering the telephone
- The process for greeting a patient
- The process for organizing patient files

Thus, a process is the step-by-step way of doing something over time. Considered as a whole, these processes are a system:

- The on-time scheduling system
- The telephone answering system
- The patient greeting system
- The file organization system

Instead of managing people, then, the truly effective manager has been taught a system for managing a process through which people get things done.

More precisely, managers and their people, *together*, manage the processes—the systems—that comprise your business. Management is less about *who* gets things done in your business than about *how* things get done.

In fact, great managers are not fascinated with people, but with how things get done through people. Great managers are masters at figuring out how to get things done effectively and efficiently through people using extraordinary systems.

Great managers constantly ask key questions, such as:

- What is the result we intend to produce?
- Are we producing that result every single time?
- If we're not producing that result every single time, why not?
- If we're producing that result every single time, how could we produce even better results?
- Do we lack a system? If so, what would that system look like if we were to create it?
- If we have a system, why aren't we using it?

And so forth.

In short, a great manager can leave the office fully assured that it will run at least as well as it does when he or she is physically in the room.

Great managers are those who use a great management system. A system that shouts, "This is *how* we manage here." Not "This is *who* manages here."

In a truly effective practice, how you manage is always more important than who manages. Provided a system is in place, how you manage is transferable, whereas who manages isn't. *How* you manage can be taught, whereas *who* manages can't be taught.

When a practice is dependent on *who* manages—Katie, Kim, or Kevin—that business is in serious jeopardy. Because when Katie, Kim, or Kevin leaves, that business has to start over again. What an enormous waste of time and resources!

Even worse, when a practice is dependent on *who* manages, you can bet all the managers in that business are doing their own thing. What could be more unproductive than ten managers who each manage in a unique way? How in the world could you possibly manage those managers?

The answer is: You can't. Because it takes you right back to trying to manage *people* again.

And, as I hope you now know, that's impossible.

In this chapter, I often refer to managers in the plural. I know that most veterinarians only have one manager—the office manager. And so you may be thinking that a management system isn't so important in a small veterinary practice. After all, the office manager does whatever an office manager does (and thank God, because you don't want to do it).

But if your practice is ever going to turn into the business it could become, and if that business is ever going to turn into the enterprise of your dreams, then the questions you ask about how the office manager manages your affairs are critical ones. Because until you come to grips with your dual role as owner and key employee, and the relationship your manager has to those two roles, your practice/business/enterprise will never realize its potential. Thus, the need for a management system.

Management System

What, then, is a management system?

The E-Myth says that a management system is the method by which every manager innovates, quantifies, orchestrates, and then monitors the systems through which your practice produces the results you expect.

According to the E-Myth, a manager's job is simple: *A manager's job is to invent the systems through which the owner's vision is consistently and faithfully manifested at the operating level of the business.*

Which brings us right back to the purpose of your business and the need for an entrepreneurial vision.

Are you beginning to see what I'm trying to share with you? That your business is one single thing? And that all the subjects we're discussing here—money, planning, management, and so on—are all about doing one thing well?

That one thing is the one thing your practice is intended to do: distinguish your veterinary practice from all others.

It is the manager's role to make certain it all fits. And it's your role as entrepreneur to make sure your manager knows what the business is supposed to look, act, and feel like when it's finally done. As clearly as you know how, you must convey to your manager what you know to be true—your vision, your picture of the business when it's finally done. In this way, your vision is translated into your manager's marching orders every day he or she reports to work.

Unless that vision is embraced by your manager, you and your people will suffer from the tyranny of routine. And your business will suffer from it, too.

Now let's move on to *people*. Because, as we know, it's people who are causing all our problems. But before we do, let's discover what Peter has to say about management. ✤

CHAPTER

8

Don't Worry, We'll Manage

Peter Weinstein, DVM, MBA

That's been one of my mantras—focus and simplicity. Simple can be harder than complex: You have to work hard to get your thinking clean to make it simple. But it's worth it in the end because once you get there, you can move mountains.

—Steve Jobs

As a veterinary technician, I frequently answered my staff's questions with: "Don't worry, we'll manage." Suzie called in sick today; we are short a kennel person: *Don't worry, we'll manage*. Ellen didn't write down the appointment and now we have three people waiting to see you *right now: Don't worry, we'll manage*. The oxygen tanks are low and we have four anesthetic procedures to do today: *Don't worry, we'll manage*. Need I continue?

What does *we'll manage* mean when you, as a veterinarian, are the technician, manager, and entrepreneur? It meant to me: Get me into an exam room or surgery suite soon, I am much more comfortable there and maybe, just maybe, all of these hassles will go away or solve themselves, or rarely, somebody else will step in and solve them.

As a young business owner, I spent 75 percent of my time doing the technical work needed to make the clients happy and the patients healthy. One percent was spent trying to figure out where we were headed and how would we accomplish my vision. The final 24 percent was spent herding cats.

As noted previously, veterinary practices have a lot of moving parts—people parts, technology parts, animal parts. It is well documented that the greatest challenge to practice success is the people. More specifically, managing people. A.k.a., herding cats.

Besides people management, there was technology management, physical plant management, case management, financial management, and a plethora of other managements needed to make a successful practice. Herding cats! Herding cats! Herding cats!

The vision existed, but how to get there was the challenge. I tried to do it all by myself and when there wasn't enough time, I hired a doctor so I had more time to manage. And when I found things in the management world that I really didn't like, I hired a manager to manage the things that I didn't want to manage. None of this got me any closer to having a smooth-running machine. In fact, all it did was give me one more layer and additional expenses to worry about. *Argh!* I had made every mistake that Michael identified in the previous chapter. Where was this book when I was up to my ears in cat litter? We weren't managing the business, the business was managing us!

As I began to understand the E-Myth System, it dawned on me that we really did need to get the processes and systems lined out and organized. I realized that managing people was far more complicated than just assigning tasks. Managing people meant managing personalities, generational differences, psychographic differences, emotional instabilities, boyfriends, girlfriends, money issues, legal issues, childcare issues, tattoos, piercings, and attitudes. And integrating all of these diversities into a practice staff was exhausting. The practice would be so much easier if we didn't need people, wouldn't it?

So how about integrating the systems and the accountabilities and outcomes and benchmarks and letting the people do the work needed to achieve the outcomes? Instead of managing the people, let the people develop the systems and run the systems and just focus on managing the systems instead? What if the whole product was a series of interchangeable people who could run the system so it is not dependent upon just one person to get things done? Sound like utopia? Well, that became my goal in my practice.

Managing to Get There

Stop thinking like the management prophets who you read and listen to, and think from a systems standpoint. As a health-care provider, you understand organ systems and the concept of everything working together with associated communications and feedback systems in the body. Each organ has a goal and a process by which it accomplishes each goal. Some organs have multiple goals: the pancreas has an exocrine and an endocrine process that have different functions. This is like having an exam room component and a surgery component to your practice. They exist independently and codependently. Each organ system has as its ultimate goal and primary aim to keep the body alive, pain-free, and comfortable. In a business, each system has processes that *must* intimately integrate into accomplishing the primary aim or vision of the practice. No practice system should be independent of the ultimate vision. Although each system will be composed of independent, stand-alone processes, they all have a common goal.

If your body had to think about each system by itself and independently manage each organ, it would be completely dysfunctional. For the most part, your practice is a dysfunctional body: individual people doing individual tasks to earn a paycheck. In a systems-driven practice, people can be interchangeable parts that, by referencing an operations manual, step in and help out. Imagine if the heart could step in and help a failing kidney.

Building the Operations Manuals to deliver the primary aim is foundational to E-Myth success. Once you have the various operations manuals you need—front desk, exam room, treatment room, kennels, financial—you can now manage to the outcomes delineated in the manuals. It then becomes the operational processes that drive your success, not the people. And then, when you have an issue, you don't have it with a person, you have it with a system. Manage the systems and *not* the people. Wow! Novel!

Instead of having managers who do the things you really don't want to do—things such as hiring, firing, reviews, ordering, servicing equipment—you have systems in place to follow that guide you in hiring, firing, counseling, ordering, servicing equipment. And anybody can step in and do them, so you only have to manage systems.

If you do all that, you have a good practice with processes and systems. It's when you understand that a good practice needs also to be a good business, and that just being busy doesn't make you a good business. When your systems are replicable, repeatable, and deliverable by virtually anyone—including, and most importantly, the owner—you are on your way to a successful business and enterprise. Until you get there, there is a lot of motion, some action, and a predominance of chaos.

Manager's Roles

Since healthcare delivery is a perpetually changing environment, your managers must consistently innovate the systems you have in place, modifying and updating the old, or, with the help of the staff, adding new systems and processes to accomplish the needed tasks. Systems do not sit still—systems change and systems support the primary aim of the practice. A manager's first role in an E-Myth practice: constantly work with the staff to innovate the systems.

If you don't measure it, you can't manage it. So, role number two of a manager in this practice is to quantify the results. Daily, weekly, monthly, quarterly, semi-annual, and annual key performance indicators (KPIs) are collected and reviewed to determine in which direction the practice is heading relative to its goals and benchmarks. Systems are changed if the variation is too great. The KPIs provide a status update so the ship can be steered before it hits the major storm.

The third role for the manager in a systems environment is to get the cats singing the same song, metaphorically. Remember, people are the bane to a systems success on one hand, and necessary on the other. The manager orchestrates the people so that instead of a cacophony of sound, you have a mellifluous melody.

The manager, with staff in tow, now documents the processes that comprise the systems that populate the Operations Manual. Then, instead of coaxing, cajoling, motivating, and praying the staff accomplishes the desired outcomes, the manager orchestrates the operational systems to accomplish the established goals, all the while updating the needed systems. It is this concept of a management system—managing the systems that are optimally delivered by the staff—that differentiates a systematized practice and creates an exceptional client and patient experience.

If you haven't yet figured it out, the entire management system can exist independent of any one individual. All of a sudden, your practice's success isn't dependent upon you, your manager, your head receptionist, and your technicians. It is dependent upon the systems you have created, including:

- Receptionist Hiring System
- Technician Onboarding System
- New Client Welcoming System
- Dog Neuter Surgery System
- Post Boarding Release System

The Receptionist Hiring System refers to a job description that clearly delineates the qualities needed for that position. And that job description fits into an organizational chart so that the new hire knows who to go to when there are questions that need to be answered about the computers, files, or pharmacy.

It is all an inherently integrated system that runs as smoothly as a Swiss watch, never needing more than a quick winding every once in awhile. Veterinary medicine has long been a doctor-driven practice, but it is morphing to a client- and patient-driven business. What it needs to strive for is a purpose-driven practice.

And you, as the technician, manager, entrepreneur, can function equally as strong in each area because you have the right systems in place. Notice, I didn't say the right *people*. That is much harder to predict. The right *systems* are predictable, repeatable, and consistent. Something people never will be.

Speaking of people, that is the next area Michael will give us his insights on. I can't wait for this chapter, since businesses that rely on people are the unluckiest businesses in the world. But how can we operate without people? Michael, enlighten us! ✦

CHAPTER

9

On the Subject of People

Michael E. Gerber

Very few people go to the doctor when they have a cold. They go to the theatre instead.

—Oscar Wilde

Every veterinarian whom I have ever met has complained to me about people.

About employees: "They come in late, they go home early, they have the focus of an antique camera!"

About clients: "They want the most cutting-edge treatment for pennies!"

People, people, people: every veterinarian's nemesis. And at the heart of it all are the people who work for you.

"By the time I tell them how to do it, I could have done it twenty times myself!" "How come nobody listens to what I say?" "Why is it nobody ever does what I ask them to do?" Does this sound like you?

So what's the problem with people? To answer that, think back to the last time you walked into a veterinarian's office. What did you see in the people's faces?

Most people working in veterinary practices are harried. You can see it in their expressions. They're negative. They're bad-spirited. They're humorless. And with good reason. After all, they're surrounded by people with sick or dying pets, who are counted as family members to them. Patients are looking for nurturing, for empathy, for care. And many are either terrified or depressed. They don't want to be there.

Is it any wonder employees at most veterinary practices are disgruntled? They're surrounded by unhappy people all day. They're answering the same questions 24/7. And most of the time, the veterinarian has no time for them. He or she is too busy leading a dysfunctional life.

Working with people brings great joy—and monumental frustration. And so it is with veterinarians and their people. But why? And what can we do about it?

Let's look at the typical veterinarian—who this person is and isn't.

Most veterinarians are unprepared to use other people to get results. Not because they can't find people, but because they are fixated on getting the results themselves. In other words, most veterinarians are not the businesspeople they need to be, but *technicians suffering from an entrepreneurial seizure*.

Am I talking about you? What were you doing before you became an entrepreneur?

Were you a hired technician working for a large multi-location practice? A midsized practice? A small practice?

Didn't you imagine owning your own practice as the way out?

Didn't you think that because you knew how to do the technical work—because you knew so much about research, diagnosis, and treatment modalities—that you were automatically prepared to create a practice that does that type of work?

Didn't you figure that by creating your own practice, you could dump the boss once and for all? How else to get rid of that impossible person, the one driving you crazy, the one who never let you do your own thing, the one who was the main reason you decided to take the leap into a business of your own in the first place?

Didn't you start your own practice so that you could become your own boss?

And didn't you imagine that once you became your own boss, you would be free to do whatever you wanted to do—and to take home all the money?

Honestly, isn't that what you imagined? So you went into business for yourself and immediately dived into work.

Doing it, doing it, doing it.

Busy, busy, busy.

Until one day you realized (or maybe not) that you were doing all of the work. You were doing everything you knew how to do, plus a lot more you knew nothing about. Building sweat equity, you thought.

In reality, a technician suffering from an entrepreneurial seizure.

You were just hoping to make a buck in your own practice. And sometimes you did earn a wage. But other times you didn't. You were the one signing the checks, all right, but they went to other people.

Does this sound familiar? Is it driving you crazy?

Well, relax, because we're going to show you the right way to do it this time.

Read carefully. Be mindful of the moment. You are about to learn the secret you've been waiting for all your working life.

The People Law

It's critical to know this about the working life of veterinarians who own their own veterinary practice: *Without people, you don't own a practice, you own a job.* And it can be the worst job in the world because you're working for a lunatic! (Nothing personal—but we have to face facts.)

Let me state what every veterinarian knows: Without people, you're going to have to do it all yourself. Without human help, you're doomed to try to do too much. This isn't a breakthrough idea, but it's amazing how many veterinarians ignore the truth. They end up knocking themselves out, ten to twelve hours a day. They try to do more, but less actually gets done.

The load can double you over and leave you panting. In addition to the work you're used to doing, you may also have to do the books. And the organizing. And the filing. You'll have to do the planning and the scheduling. When you own your own practice, the daily minutiae are never-ceasing—as I'm sure you've found out. Like painting the Golden Gate Bridge: it's endless. Which puts it beyond the realm of human possibility. Until you discover how to get it done by somebody else, it will continue on and on until you're a burned-out husk.

But with others helping you, things will start to drastically improve. If, that is, you truly understand how to engage people in the work you need them to do. When you learn how to do that, when you learn how to replace yourself with other people—people trained in your system—then your practice can really begin to grow. Only then will you begin to experience true freedom yourself.

What typically happens is that veterinarians, knowing they need help answering the phone, filing, and so on, go out and find people who can do these things. Once they delegate these duties, however, they rarely spend any time with the employee. Deep down they feel it's not important how these things get done; it's only important that they get done.

They fail to grasp the requirement for a system that makes people their greatest asset rather than their greatest liability. A system so reliable that if Chris dropped dead tomorrow, Leslie could do exactly what Chris did. That's where the People Law comes in.

The People Law says that each time you add a new person to your practice using an intelligent (turnkey) system that works, you expand your reach. And you can expand your reach almost infinitely! People allow you to be everywhere you want to be simultaneously, without actually having to be there in the flesh.

People are to a veterinarian what a record was to Frank Sinatra. A Sinatra record could be (and still is) played in a million places at the same time, regardless of where Frank was. And every record sale produced royalties for Sinatra (or his estate).

With the help of other people, Sinatra created a quality recording that faithfully replicated his unique talents, then made sure it was marketed and distributed, and the revenue managed.

Your people can do the same thing for you. All you need to do is to create a "recording"—a system—of your unique talents, your special way of practicing veterinary medicine, and then replicate it, market it, distribute it, and manage the revenue.

Isn't that what successful businesspeople do? Make a "recording" of their most effective ways of doing business? In this way, they provide a turnkey solution to their patients' problems. A system solution that really works.

Doesn't your practice offer the same potential for you that records did for Sinatra (and now for his heirs)? The ability to produce income without having to go to work every day?

Isn't that what your people could be for you? The means by which your system for practicing veterinary medicine could be faithfully replicated?

But first you have to have a system. You have to create a unique way of doing business that you can teach to your people, that you can manage faithfully, and that you can replicate consistently, just like McDonald's.

Because without such a system, without such a "recording," without a unique way of doing business that really works, all you're left with is people doing their own thing. And that is almost always a recipe for chaos. Rather than guaranteeing consistency, it encourages mistake after mistake after mistake.

And isn't that how the problem started in the first place? People doing whatever *they* perceived they needed to do, regardless of what you wanted? People left to their own devices, with no regard for the costs of their behavior? The costs to you?

In other words, people without a system.

Can you imagine what would have happened to Frank Sinatra if he had followed that example? If every one of his recordings had been done differently? Imagine a million different versions of "My Way." It's unthinkable.

Would you buy a record like that? What if Frank were having a bad day? What if he had a sore throat?

Please hear this: The People Law is unforgiving. Without a systematic way of doing business, people are more often a liability than an asset. Unless you prepare, you'll find out too late which ones are which.

The People Law says that without a specific system for doing business; without a specific system for recruiting, hiring, and training your people to use that system; and without a specific system for managing and improving your systems, your practice will always be a crapshoot.

Do you want to roll the dice with your practice at stake? Unfortunately, that is what most veterinarians are doing.

The People Law also says that you can't effectively delegate your responsibilities unless you have something specific to delegate. And that something specific is a way of doing business that works!

Sinatra is gone, but his voice lives on. And someone is still counting his royalties. That's because Sinatra had a system that worked.

Do you? Let's see if Peter does, and then we will move on to the subject of associate veterinarians. ✤

CHAPTER 10

Your Staff: Herding Cats

Peter Weinstein, DVM, MBA

With great power comes great responsibility.

—Voltaire

In my opinion, this is the most important chapter of this book. The delivery of small animal veterinary business is so people-dependent that you cannot separate the success of your practice, business, and enterprise from your success in working with the people who deliver the service and care. Of course, they never teach you that in veterinary school.

As a clinician working for somebody else, I never really knew nor understood all of the dynamics of managing people. I was involved at various levels of training, co-existing, and coaching co-workers but they weren't "my problem."

I, as the technician-turned-entrepreneur, hired two young, but experienced assistants to get us up and running. We added a groomer to provide some ancillary business and to draw clients. When you are seeing just a handful of people every day, things aren't too bad. Erica showed up to open the practice in the morning. Laura showed up later to help Erica and to close up things at night. Cari did her grooming thing. I was the doctor, manager, entrepreneur, inventory specialist, staff scheduler, trainer, bookkeeper, toilet paper purchaser, and a billion other things. And it was okay…for a while.

Then Cari had boyfriend problems and would call in sick, or not even call in. So we had to make up excuses for her clients, which, of course, reflected negatively on the business. The groomer who was supposed to be an asset became a liability. We had no replacement or system in place to handle her absence. We were too dependent upon her as a person and not the responsibilities of the position.

Erica and Laura came with their own set of issues. Whether it was enlarged tonsils or other medical conditions that influenced their ability to work, I found myself not only being the technician-entrepreneur-manager, but also the receptionist, kennel person, and more than once, the bather/groomer. I would show up to a business that wasn't open for business because somebody was too sick to come in or to even call. And as much as the parts were very interchangeable, they were also necessary to get the work done. The people were so integral to running the business that when they weren't there, the only one who had the institutional knowledge was . . . me! Not good. An owner- and individual-dependent business survives tenuously at best.

I loved my staff, except when I didn't. You can never prepare yourself for the people portion of being an entrepreneur. But we continued to grow in spite of ourselves. And started to develop a good reputation, in spite of ourselves. And we added new variables to the staff. Ah, the human dynamic creates quite a challenge to the psyche. I thought I was a pretty good clinician, but I learned I was a very inexperienced manager, leader, and boss.

As a technician, I focused on patient care and client care. I found myself avoiding the management roles by keeping busy playing doctor. So the inmates started to run the asylum. I hired some very skilled people. People who had worked at other veterinary hospitals. Even people who I had worked with at other practices. However, hiring people for their skills didn't always work. I didn't realize how important the practice culture was and how skills can be taught, but personality can't. The practice became a revolving door of people who had the capabilities but not the character to fulfill my primary aim, nor work with the others chosen to accomplish the aim. To quote Mr. Spock, I was learning "The needs of the many outweigh the needs of the few or the one." But how do you build a successful business that is so dependent upon people?

A System Is the Solution

According to Michael, "The People Law states that without a systematic way of doing business, people are more often a liability than an asset."

I couldn't agree more.

When I had my E-Myth epiphany, I realized that I needed to rethink how we did things. Job descriptions, checklists, how-we-do-it-here forms, and training all became integrated into the operations of the practice. Staff started to become empowered to be problem solvers and to take responsibility and accountability for their actions. I posted the following sign in multiple places:

"You are more likely to receive forgiveness than permission."

This was the initial stage of my adding processes and systems to my practice, and it started to work. I found myself less responsible for every little thing, and had people accountable to complete the processes needed to get the work done and the business moving closer to the goals. But I still wasn't fully releasing the reins and letting the horse run (note another animal metaphor).

What would it take to let go and allow things to happen? Later on in my life, as a consultant and studier of human interactions, I realized that the reason that most veterinarians do not delegate nor release has everything to do with trust. And the lack of trust comes from lack of training. I still didn't completely trust my staff and, thus, was too much of a helicopter boss.

The Game of Telephone

Training in most veterinary practices is the game of telephone. In the beginning, mine was no exception.

Do you remember the kid's game of telephone? A bunch of kids sit in a circle, one kid is given a few sentences to share with the person next to him, who shares it with the person next to them, and on and on. The last person is asked what the message is that he received. By the time it gets around the circle, the final message isn't anything like the original message.

And so it goes with hiring and training new staff. Without a system in place, the longest-term employee becomes the trainer for the newest employee. The newest employee is replacing the employee who is now leaving, and she becomes the next trainer. With no written policies, procedures, or protocols, it becomes the game of telephone and before you know it, the vision and training you originally had in mind is completely unidentifiable. With no understanding of your primary aim, your highly regarded staff does what they want to, leading to chaos.

The Training System

Education and training are an asset, not a liability. Training to a level of trust allows people to grow and develop. A lack of training encourages stagnation, and staff then becomes space-occupying lesions, taking up room but never contributing. Never becoming engaged. Just doing tasks.

We integrated a learning system of:

- Biweekly staff education programs
- Paid-for continuing education programs

- Self-training by trying
- Access to training resources—CDs, DVDs, books

And it was all documented and chronicled and accessible.

Provide the tools and the trust, and your staff will build your hospital. The people then expand your reach and ability to generate income by doing those things that are not dependent upon the DVM. Most veterinary-practice acts clearly define what *must* be done by licensed people (technicians, doctors). Guess what? Everything else can be done by everyone else. If trained to a level of trust. If held accountable. And if the processes are integrated into a system whereby anybody can step in and do it. You can stop doing it, doing it, doing it, and let others grow concurrently. And that leaves more time for the primary income-generating functions of the veterinarian that include:

- Complete physical examinations
- Surgery
- Client engagement and trust building
- Envisioning the final practice product

People without a system are a liability, and I will vouch for that. People with a system are a profitable practice, business, enterprise.

Controlling the Chaos

Once I learned that human resource management and herding cats were synonymous, I recognized that there had to be a better way. The E-Myth system helped me to understand the concept of creating the processes and the systems, and letting the people run the systems. The key was creating a systems-dependent business that was not as people-dependent.

Now the challenge was two-fold: document the processes and populate the day-to-day operational and training systems, while concurrently creating a hiring system.

The Hiring System

During the early stages of my practice, my hiring system was one of resume review, calling references, one-on-one interviews, working interviews, and job offers. There was no real system, just a gut feeling. What was I looking for from the applicant? I have no idea . . . a pulse? Of course, calling references was futile most of the time. The one-on-one interview had no set questions and found me selling the job rather than listening to the candidate try to sell him or herself. The working interview had its value because the rest of the staff could get their feel for the individual. And, of course, once they were hired . . . well, between the game of telephone and trial and error, the candidate either sank or swam.

The Hiring System, although it should have been one of the early systems that we created, became the cure to future hiring errors. Starting with the classifieds, through each step of the process, the hiring staff had a recipe for success. It became more formalized and more integrated into the needs of the staff and the practice. Of course, mistakes were made. The person who interviews isn't always the person who shows up for the job on day one. But the process became less painful, and the product much more predictable.

The Hiring System includes the benchmarks, job descriptions, and expectations and standards for new hires. The values, behaviors, personality, and motivators for new hires can weigh more heavily than the skills that they pretend to have. The system ensures you find, train, retain, and develop the best people for the position. People who will deliver the client and patient experience you have envisioned and will stay for the experience and work environment more than they ever will for the money.

And of course, the systems idea was the foundation for everything. And with the systems in place, hiring a manager was easier. Her job became to oversee the systems and monitor the people who were working the systems. I didn't have to do it all by myself any longer. And I could now start to think about making the practice less and less dependent upon me.

Some Thoughts in Summary

As noted at the beginning of this section, I think that this is the most important chapter of this book. Veterinarians went to veterinary school to work with animals. Many veterinary staff work for veterinary hospitals because they get to work with animals. However, it is the people who bring their pets in and the people who care for them who make veterinary medicine a business. You can't ignore the people and their inherent challenges.

So this chapter on herding cats carries with it some significant messages:

1. Having systems in place creates a business that is less people-dependent and more systems-dependent. Yes, you need people to run the systems, but you can find people who fit your business culture and support your primary aim and teach them what they lack in skills. In a patient-centered practice, your people are responsible to the system and the associated processes as defined in their job description or position description. Systems run the business, and people run the systems.
2. Archimedes said it millennia ago: *Give me a lever long enough and a fulcrum on which to place it, and I shall move the world.* Learning to delegate and leverage your staff will allow the clinician to be clinician, the manager to be manager, and the entrepreneur to have time to look down the road to success. Train to a level of trust and grow an engaged, people-centered practice. Let your staff be successful, and they will help you become successful.
3. Training systems are a must. The technical skills are a small part. The most important skills, those that you will be hiring for, are the communication skills. Teaching people how to say something—the so-called people skills—is the difference maker. Hiring for EQ (emotional intelligence) vs. IQ will make your practice stand out in the community. Training doesn't stop after thirty, sixty or

ninety days. An ongoing training system ensures continual growth and success.

4. Create a hiring system that ensures the right people in the right seats on the bus (Jim Collins, *Good to Great*). From recruiting through training and developing, employees are given a road map to success through The Hiring System and the other organized systems that support the business model. This system should make sure you are always staffed appropriately to meet the needs of your clients and patients. In a well-systematized practice, The Hiring System lets you take your time to find the right people. The clinician/manager always staffs based upon the budget, and thus are slow to hire. The entrepreneur DVM hires proactively to meet projected needs. Oh, and by the way, the system allows you to cut your losses early. No more collections of staff dead on the job but not yet buried.
5. Your people are your greatest asset. Treat them as such.

It is interesting: this entire chapter focused on the non-professional people systems. What about the professionals, the staff who are part of your exit strategy, or at least your time-management strategy? Let's see what Michael has to say about associates. ✤

CHAPTER

11

On the Subject of Associates

Michael E. Gerber

Associate yourself with men of good quality if you esteem your own reputation, for 'tis better to be alone than in bad company.

—George Washington

If you're a sole practitioner—that is, you're selling only yourself—then your veterinary practice, called a *sole proprietorship*, will never make the leap to a veterinary practice called a *business*. The progression from sole proprietorship to business to enterprise demands that you hire other veterinarians to do what you do (or don't do). Contractors call these people subcontractors; for our purposes, we'll refer to them as associates.

Contractors know that subs can be a huge problem. It's no less true for veterinarians. Until you face this special business problem, your practice will never become a business, and your business will certainly never become an enterprise.

Long ago, God said, "Let there be veterinarians. And so they never forget who they are in my creation, let them be damned forever to hire people exactly like themselves." Enter the associates.

Merriam-Webster's Collegiate Dictionary, Eleventh Edition, defines *sub* as "under, below, secretly; inferior to." If associate veterinarians are like sub-veterinarians, you could define an associate as "an inferior individual contracted to perform part or all of another's contract."

In other words, you, the veterinarian, make a conscious decision to hire someone "inferior" to yourself to fulfill your commitment to your patients and clients, for which you are ultimately and solely liable.

Why in the world do we do these things to ourselves? Where will this madness lead? It seems the blind are leading the blind, and the blind are paying others to do it. And when a veterinarian is blind, you know there's a problem!

It's time to step out of the darkness and come into the light. Forget about being Mr. Nice Guy—it's time to do things that work.

Solving the Associate Veterinarian Problem

Let's say you're about to hire an associate veterinarian. Someone who has specific skills: technician, rehab, whatever. It all starts with choosing the right personnel. After all, these are people to whom you are delegating your responsibility and for whose behavior you are completely liable. Do you really want to leave that choice to chance? Are you that much of a gambler? I doubt it.

If you've never worked with your new associate, how do you really know he or she is skilled? For that matter, what does *skilled* mean?

For you to make an intelligent decision about this staff member, you must have a working definition of the word skilled. Your challenge is to know exactly what your expectations are, then to make sure your other veterinarians operate with precisely the same expectations. Failure here almost ensures a breakdown in your relationship.

I want you to write the following on a piece of paper: "By skilled, I mean . . ." Once you create your personal definition, it will become a standard for you and your practice, for your patients, and for your associate veterinarians.

A standard, according to *Merriam-Webster's Collegiate Dictionary, Eleventh Edition*, is something "set up and established by authority as a rule for the measure of quantity, weight, extent, value, or quality."

Thus, your goal is to establish a measure of quality control, a standard of skill, which you will apply to all your associate veterinarians. More importantly, you are also setting a standard for the performance of your practice.

By creating standards for your selection of other veterinarians—standards of skill, performance, integrity, financial stability, and experience—you have begun the powerful process of building a practice that can operate exactly as you expect it to.

By carefully thinking about exactly what to expect, you have already begun to improve your practice.

In this enlightened state, you will see the selection of your associates as an opportunity to define what you (1) intend to provide for your patients, (2) expect from your employees, and (3) demand for your life.

Powerful stuff, isn't it? Are you up to it? Are you ready to feel your rising power?

Don't rest on your laurels just yet. Defining those standards is only the first step you need to take. The second step is to create an *associate veterinarian development system*.

An associate veterinarian development system is an action plan designed to tell you what you are looking for in an associate. It includes the exact benchmarks, accountabilities, timing of fulfillment, and budget you will assign to the process of looking for associate veterinarians, identifying them, recruiting them, interviewing them, training them, managing their work, auditing their performance, compensating them, reviewing them regularly, and terminating or rewarding them for their performance.

All of these things must be documented—actually *written down*—if they're going to make any difference to you, your associate veterinarians, your managers, or your bank account!

And then you've got to persist with that system, come hell or high water. Just as Ray Kroc did. Just as Walt Disney did. Just as Sam Walton did.

This leads us to our next topic of discussion: the subject of estimating. But first, let's find out what Peter has to say on the subject of associate veterinarians. ✤

CHAPTER

12

A Pain in the Ass-ociate . . . Or Not

Peter Weinstein, DVM, MBA

If you want to go fast, go alone. If you want to go far, go together.

—African Proverb

There are many times during the life of a small business that your blood pressure elevates into the danger zone. One of those is when you add your first healthcare professional to work beside you or in your absence. Your so-called associate is added to your staff to take the burden off your endless schedule of seeing clients, paying bills, hiring staff, ensuring appropriate inventory. They are positioned to be you when you can't be you. But they aren't you, and that is a problem. Unless you have a methodology to make them . . . you!

I added my first associate as a part-time solution to burnout and not enough time to get everything done. And when I mean everything, I mean *everything*. I was the technician, manager, and entrepreneur and just couldn't juggle all of the balls. Rather than pass the management ball, I passed some of the technician balls. My highly seasoned, highly skilled associate filled in so I could get out. The operations manual was in its infancy and the hiring process went just like this:

"Hey Doc, do you have time to cover for me two days a week?"

"Sure, but it depends which days."

"Which days are you available?"

"Tuesdays and Thursdays."

"Those days."

"Great."

"Can you start tomorrow?"

Something like that. There was no hiring system. No education on how we did things. No discussions on medical record keeping. Just, when can you start? It worked out okay. She wasn't that busy; the clients liked her. And I got the time I needed to do what I needed to and not burn out too much more.

By the time, I was ready to add a full-time associate, operations were becoming more standardized, and I had enough confidence in my clinical capabilities and myself that I had some standards of care that I could use as a foundation for any new professional hires. Again, I sought out somebody I knew and who had a similar practice philosophy. With an idea in mind, we were able to integrate him into our system fairly easily. He spent time in the exam room with me watching my approach, and I did similarly. He spent time with the staff learning how they did things and vice versa. We had a mutual admiration society. And best of all, he liked to do the things that I really hated to do. It was win-win-win.

As the teamwork made the dream work, we looked to add another associate. This time it would be a younger doctor, one who needed mentoring and coaching, but one who fit in with the clinical foundation we had established. Through a series of amazing events, we found the right person. And this time, we had a plan.

Our New Doctor Training System ensured a slow assimilation of our young associate into the way we did things—medical records, patient care, client service. And it integrated the staff at all levels into the training program to ensure a mutual respect between the professional and para-professional staff. It also took the burden of training off the professional staff and left it to the staff to show her the ropes. It worked!

As a hospital owner, I was very fortunate that my professional hiring process, which was very unscientific and lacked any logic to it, worked. Gut feeling and risk-taking had its place in this process. However, this isn't always the way. And there is no way that a successful small business can use smoke and mirrors to build its professional staff, and ensure success and longevity for all parties.

Before you even think about adding a professional to your staff, there is a financial evaluation that must take place to determine if you can truly afford to add a new expense, and heavy one at that. (Of course, in some cases the mental needs exceed the financial wherewithal, and self-sacrifices are necessary to avoid total burnout and collapse.)

If the dollars and cents make sense, then you need the appropriate job descriptions, benchmarks, goals, and expectations clearly delineated. You have to envision the best person and the best skills that are required to ensure a successful hire, not just for a job, but for a career and—in a perfect world—a succession plan. Hiring a healthcare professional should never be an act of desperation.

Your Professional Hiring Process will be used to match suitors to the position and the practice. It should include a thorough evaluation of the candidate by all stakeholders—other veterinarians, technical staff, client service staff, animal care staff and...clients. Have a professional work some shifts and see some clients. You can only be on your best behavior for so long. The skeletons come out of the closet soon enough when the pressure's on. If the right person is found—and only if the right person is found—can you move to the next phase of the Associate System, the Onboarding and Integration Process.

An experienced, seasoned veterinarian can routinely step in and handle most of the medical conditions that are routinely seen. The standards of care may vary, the medication options may differ, but the case management is pretty textbook. Although this is an issue, it isn't the issue.

It's the people skills that are the issue. You can teach the technical/clinical work, but you really can't hire an introverted, self-absorbed narcissist and convert them into a gregarious, caring schmoozer. The Hiring Process should help screen for this; the Onboarding and Integration Process will truly expose the shortcomings, and hopefully do so early on.

The formal onboarding process will include a series of benchmarks of success, from a management, clinical, and people skills standpoint. A formal ninety-day, step-by-step training and coaching program can take even the most green veterinarian and give him the confidence needed to be a great clinician, and more importantly a great team player. There is no rush to put a young veterinarian into the fire. Remember, we are looking for a career hire, not a job hire. The training process should ensure a successful professional.

As a part of the life cycle of the associate, there should also be a series of financial benchmarks that indicate the growth of the person as a clinician and educator of pet owners on the pet's needs. Personal and clinical growth leads to financial growth and a contribution to the financial success of the practice and the practitioner. In other words, the associate makes more money for himself or herself as they make more money for the practice. And the only way to do that is to make sure that the staff that they work with supports them. Why do I know this? Here's a brief story:

As a consultant, I was working for a one-doctor practice owned by a successful veterinarian with great people skills and a very dedicated, devoted, and skilled staff. She had grown to a point financially and personally that she needed some help and, with no process in place, hired a young but experienced veterinarian to cover for her a few days per week.

On the surface, things looked good for a few weeks. After a month or two, the owner noted that the days she returned to the practice after her days off were absolutely insanely busy. She also noted that the days she wasn't there the appointment book was becoming more and more sparsely filled.

It got to a point that she hated taking time off because when she got back it was so out of control. On the other hand, the young associate was seeing fewer and fewer people. Nobody on the staff mentioned anything to the owner.

Finally, after about four months of increasing frustration, the owner asked the manager what was going on. The manager was quite candid. She noted that the staff didn't want to upset the owner because they realized how burdened she was. But they all hated the associate. The associate completely disrespected the staff and treated them as subhuman primates. The feeling was reflected back to the associate. In addition, the staff really didn't trust the clinical judgment of the associate. On the days that she was working, if phone calls came in and the appointment couldn't wait until the owner came back, they were sending appointments to other hospitals in the area. Oh, and the associate was receiving bonuses on her production, so if she didn't see any clients, she didn't get a bonus. And the staff knew this. Welcome to my nightmare!

As noted earlier, the growth of your business is a good news/bad news situation. The good news is you're making more money; the bad news is the number of problems that arise magnifies. As you add staff, you start to lose control. As you add more systems and processes, you add control. And in any team dynamic, as you add more people, you set back a few steps the dynamic setting of your systems as everybody learns the system and integrates into the practice. That is for the para-professional staff.

When you add a veterinarian, the opportunities for chaos escalate. There is no question that hiring somebody to be an associate just because she has a pulse and can fog a mirror is not a solution—it is an accident waiting for a place to happen. To grow your practice on the professional side, you need to know your vision or primary aim. And make sure to:

1. Hire somebody to bring you closer to your vision.
2. Onboard and train to ensure success.
3. Integrate with the entire team and check the ego at the door.
4. Integrate with the clients via a system to validate them to the clients, thus helping develop the trust needed to be accepted.

You can only do so much on your own. When you are ready to grow your practice and go further, you need to add people—the right way!

Adding people adds more variables to the equation and, with it, more opportunities for errors in the way things are done. This makes it even more important to have a plan in mind and systems to support them. In the next chapter, Michael addresses estimating. You can call it guessing, prognosticating, or predicting. Call it what you will, this issue needs to be addressed to ensure consistency. Let's discover Michael's insights. ✤

CHAPTER

13

On the Subject of Estimating

Michael E. Gerber

The best we can do is size up the chances, calculate the risks involved, estimate our ability to deal with them, and then make our plans with confidence.

—Henry Ford

One of the greatest weaknesses of veterinarians is accurately estimating their ability to accurately diagnosis and heal an animal—preferably very quickly. *Webster's Eleventh* defines estimate as "a rough or approximate calculation." Anyone who has visited a housing renovation site knows that those estimates can be rough indeed.

Do you want to see someone who gives you a rough approximation? What if your veterinarian gave you a rough approximation on the odds your pet would survive the prescribed treatment?

The fact is that we can predict many things we don't typically predict. For example, there are ways to assess the outcome of a procedure. Look at the steps of the process. Most of the things you do are standard, so develop a step-by-step system and stick to it.

In my book *The E-Myth Manager*, I raised eyebrows by suggesting that doctors eliminate the waiting room. Why? You don't need it if you're always on time. The same goes for a veterinary practice. If you're always on time, then your patients don't have to wait.

What if a veterinarian made this promise: on time, every time, as promised, or we pay for it?

"Impossible!" veterinarians cry. "Each patient is different. We simply can't know how long each appointment will take."

Do you follow this? Since veterinarians believe they're incapable of knowing how to organize their time, they build a practice based on lack of knowing and lack of control. They build a practice based on estimates.

I once had a veterinarian ask me, "What happens when a distressed pet owner contacts us to see his animal immediately, and we discover that the pet requires an extremely time-consuming treatment and the owner is demanding we do it right away? How can we deal with that so unexpectedly?" My first thought was that it's not being dealt with now. Few veterinarians are able to give generously of their time. Ask anyone who's been to a veterinarian's office lately. It's chaos.

The solution is interest, attention, analysis. Try detailing what you do at the beginning of an interaction, what you do in the middle, and what you do at the end. How long does each take? In the absence of such detailed, quantified standards, everything ends up being an estimate, and a poor estimate at that.

However, a practice organized around a system, with adequate staff to run it, has time for proper attention. It's built right into the system.

Too many veterinarians have grown accustomed to thinking in terms of estimates without thinking about what the term really means. Is it any wonder many veterinary practices are in trouble?

Enlightened veterinarians, in contrast, banish the word estimate from their vocabulary. When it comes to estimating, just say *no*!

"But you can never be exact," veterinarians have told me for years. "Close, maybe. But never exact."

I have a simple answer to that: *You have to be*. You simply can't afford to be inexact. You can't accept inexactness in yourself or in your veterinary practice.

You can't go to work every day believing that your practice, the work you do, and the commitments you make are all too complex and unpredictable to be exact. With a mindset like that, you're doomed to run a sloppy ship. A ship that will eventually sink and suck you down with it.

This is so easy to avoid. Sloppiness—in both thought and action—is the root cause of your frustrations.

The solution to those frustrations is clarity. Clarity gives you the ability to set a clear direction, which fuels the momentum you need to grow your business.

Clarity, direction, momentum—they all come from insisting on exactness.

But how do you create exactness in a hopelessly inexact world? The answer is this. You discover the exactness in your practice by refusing to do any work that can't be controlled exactly.

The only other option is to analyze the field, determine where the opportunities are, and then organize your practice to be the exact provider of the services you've chosen to offer.

Two choices, and only two choices: (1) evaluate your practice and then limit yourself to the tasks you know you can do exactly, or (2) start all over by analyzing the field, identifying the key opportunities in that market, and building a practice that operates exactly.

What you cannot do, what you must refuse to do, from this day forward, is to allow yourself to operate with an inexact mindset. It will lead you to ruin.

Which leads us inexorably back to the word I have been using through this book: *systems*.

Who makes estimates? Only veterinarians who are unclear about exactly how to do the task in question. Only veterinarians whose experience has taught them that if something can go wrong, it will—and to them!

I'm not suggesting that a *systems solution* will guarantee that you always perform exactly as promised. But I am saying that a systems solution will faithfully alert you when you're going off track, and will do it before you have to pay the price for it.

In short, with a systems solution in place, your need to estimate will be a thing of the past, both because you have organized your practice to anticipate mistakes, and because you have put into place the system to do something about those mistakes before they blow up.

There's this, too: To make a promise you intend to keep places a burden on you and your managers to dig deeply into how you intend to keep it. Such a burden will transform your intentions and increase your attention to detail.

With the promise will come dedication. With dedication will come integrity. With integrity will come consistency. With consistency will come results you can count on. And results you can count on mean that you get exactly what you hoped for at the outset of your practice: the true pride of ownership that every veterinarian should experience.

This brings us to the subject of *patients*. Who are they? Why do they come to you? How can you identify yours? And who *should* your patients be? But first, let's see what Peter has to say about estimating. ✤

CHAPTER

14

A System Is the Solution

Peter Weinstein, DVM, MBA

Informed decision-making comes from a long tradition of guessing and then blaming others for inadequate results.

—Scott Adams

Next time you go to Starbucks, McDonald's, Marriott, Jiffy Lube, or the Ritz Carlton, watch the scientific precision that they go about handling each customer experience. Each person has a role, clearly defined, and a sequence of steps, clearly defined, to accomplish their desired outcome. Even when there is a line out of the door at 7 a.m. on a weekday, the work flow at Starbucks rarely deviates. Based upon their research, they know how to adjust the efficiency of delivery and maintain the client experience, even while people wait for their Grande Latte for $3.85 (at the time of writing).

Now, take a look at your practice. What happens when you get behind? Why did you get behind? What happens when it comes to creating a healthcare plan (estimate)? Is your client experience consistent or consistently bad? What is your average waiting time? How much are you failing to charge for because your fee schedule and estimate procedure have no fact behind them? How much inventory sits on your shelf because you guessed you needed more?

When I started my hospital, everything was random, because we had no experience upon which to build. As we grew, this randomness morphed into chaos. And this chaos created challenging experiences for the clients, patients, staff, and ultimately to the technician, manager, entrepreneur (yours truly).

My experience in the trenches parallel many of yours; my beliefs were very self-limiting and restricting my abilities to move forward and get out of the rut. In my head, there was no way I could do anything different than what my predecessors before had done. There was only one person in the way who I had to get by, and that person was me! After reading about Deming's studies in Japan, and Gerber's systems, I realized that there was a better way. I started to have a better understanding of the way services were provided in successful businesses and what would be needed to do the same in my own.

Shake Your Bottle

Inventory ordering seemed to be the first place where we could improve. We had a purchase history from the manufacturers and distributors. On the other hand, we had a sales history from our practice-management software. We could even determine seasonal fluctuations in sales and price fluctuations for our most common items. Creating an Inventory Control System was scientific, mathematical, and really didn't impose on the clinical delivery of care, nor the client experience. Unless we ran out of a product prematurely or the price went up astronomically or there was a new and better product introduced. This was an easy systems victory.

On the other hand, when it comes to the determination of fees, scheduling of appointments, and filling the surgery calendar, chaos reigned.

Some days there were too many appointments and not enough time to get all of the surgeries done. The next day, you could shoot a cannon ball through the practice and not hit an animal or client.

The F Word: FEES

Just like a dry cleaner, auto repair shop, or restaurant, veterinary medicine is a fee-for-service business. Unlike other healthcare fields, the pet insurance industry does not dictate or influence the fee schedules in the veterinary field. Wall Street, or anywhere else, does not direct us what to charge. Private practices are not even truly influenced by the corporate-owned or -operated facilities. Each practice autonomously determines what the market will bear. We have it pretty good from that standpoint. Or do we?

As a student of the sciences, I should think that the manner by which a veterinary practice operates would be scientific in nature. This means that everything done has a logical explanation. The processes are based upon measurable and tangible knowledge, and, thus, can be supported by measurable data. You would think this, wouldn't you? Keep thinking. Keep dreaming.

As I noted before, the suggested routine office call in the area of Southern California that I practiced used to be 100 times the current postage stamp rate. I somehow missed the science in that.

Additionally, many of the other fees set by a practice came from a truly statistical scientific study conducted by calling the local practices and pretending to be a consumer looking for services. The other practices' fee schedules thus determine the prevailing rate. Of course, there are national and regional fee studies that do not violate any FTC Fair Trade laws. It is all empirical.

No rate or motion studies. No price-value studies. Simply put, guess what the consumer is willing to spend and charge appropriately.

Affordable fees are great if they provide the profit needed to give you the requisite return on an annual basis, and at the time you sell. Affordable fees, if combined with value, may increase client satisfaction and minimize complaints. However, that fee also has to give value to you as the owner.

By the way, affordable is in the eyes of the beholder. So, in setting your fees you need to know your clients—psychographics *and* demographics. You need to know where the pet fits into the household and their lifestyle, while concurrently what their personal lifestyle is. Pet care is not a budgeted line item for most people, so to create a level of trust you need to know the demographics of your community and charge fair and reasonable fees. You can be the best, the highest, the most competitive, the cheapest, or wherever you want to position yourself, but remember the client makes the choice, so you must provide value for them as well as for yourself. To quote my friend Tom Cat, *no client is worse than no client!*

How do you get value for your fees? Have a Financial Policy, systems, and processes for setting fees and talking about your fees with your clients, and base your decisions on common sense and integrity. If you couldn't afford to pay for the care of your pets at your practice, if your staff couldn't afford to pay for the care of their pets at your practice, could you be charging too much?

Remember, it is all about profitability. So having systems, workflows, and an efficiently and effectively used physical plant will go a long way to impacting the expense side of the equation. The fees you charge are only one-half of the profitability equation: you need systems to impact both sides.

Bottom line: If you feel guilty when a client starts to question your fees, why? Because you don't believe in your fees and, thus, it is the technician thinking. Get over it! The entrepreneur needs the money!

Filling the Appointment Slot

Waiting for patient care is an expectation, you can tell. Clients don't bring comic books to read in the waiting room. They bring *War and Peace* or Harry Potter books. And they expect to finish them before their visit is over. Houston, we have a problem!

Beyond the pricing structure, the rest of the operations of a veterinary practice came from intensive studies to ascertain exactness. (Sarcasm!) The inefficiency of actions of veterinary practices is commonplace. Appointment books are out of control. How can some practices have ten-minute appointment times and similar practices have twenty-, thirty-, or even forty-minute appointment times? What is double-booking but an opportunity for everybody to wait? And what about the no-appointment-book practice? Isn't that just an invitation for chaos? Is there any science to the length of an appointment time so that the client experience has high value *and*, as Michael challenges, seen *on time every time?*

As a start, your vision and primary aim should be the foundation for your exam-room experience. From start to finish, you should be able to detail the step-by-step experience that the client and pet go through. Once you have envisioned that, you can put a timeline to it. And with a timeline in place, you can start to determine appointment-book time.

In looking at my own small business and visiting with hundreds of others, about 80 percent of what we make appointments for fits into about twenty categories: New Client; Puppy/Kitten visits; Routine Wellness visits; Skin check; Vomiting; Diarrhea; Itchy Skin; Itchy Ears; Young Dog Lameness; Old Dog Lameness; Urinary Tract issues; Endocrine diseases; and the list goes on.

With the list, there are variations on the theme, but as a rule, these twenty categories of appointments are predictable. With your baseline-envisioned exam-room experience as the foundation, add or subtract time, and create a list of appointment times for the most common visits. These don't change; they just get integrated into the appointment book.

With this you have a process for each type of appointment, from check-in to check-out. This is your Appointment System, and it will have a number of processes included in it, such as the check-in process, the check-out process, and so on.

Take a moment to do some time-motion studies—also known as observation—of the flow of your practice. Client and patient appointing can become more predictable if you look at what you do most often, create a step-by-step process for handling such cases, and see how much time you truly need. Take into consideration the leveraging of your staff vs. the expenditure of your time as you put this together. Remember, we are talking about the delivery of staff-based healthcare. Your staff has a responsibility for a large portion of the client experience.

With each of the top twenty cases identified, analyzed, and categorized, you can now create an appointment book process for scheduling. Personally, I like ten-minute-block appointment books. This gives you tremendous flexibility from a scheduling standpoint. A post operative recheck may be ten minutes. A new puppy or kitten, maybe forty minutes. A skin case may be thirty minutes. Diarrhea acute, maybe thirty minutes. Diarrhea chronic, maybe twenty minutes. Learning how to schedule appointments from a scientific standpoint and not a randomly assigned standpoint goes a long way to staying on time.

And you can do the same for surgery scheduling. There are only so many hours in the day that you have set aside for seeing clients, and this determines the amount of surgery time that you have. In a single-doctor practice, there is only you juggling all of this. As you add associates, the time management becomes even more challenging. Other doctors will appreciate the scientific approach to appointment and surgery scheduling, because much of the chaos will be reeled in.

Michael suggests eliminating the waiting room in his chapter. I agree with reconfiguring the waiting room but make it into a social room for clients. A place for coffee and schmoozing, because there won't be any waiting. Although I have never had anybody take up the challenge I have proposed a number of times when speaking:

Free exam for anybody waiting more than ten minutes! With a system, you can make this offer and *rarely* have to pay up.

A System Is the Solution

Really, it is!

We don't go to McDonald's for the burgers or fries. We go for the predictable experience.

We don't go to Starbucks for the coffee. We go for the experience.

Clients can go to a plethora of veterinary hospitals, but they go to yours because of the experience. If you can control that client experience by having processes and systems in place that guarantee a consistent and predictable visit, your clients will love you even more. A consistent client experience, based upon the knowledge and understanding of what you want to accomplish and, most importantly what your clients want, removes frustration and offers an exactness not found in the practices around you.

To me the following quote truly explains the reason for systems: *If you're not consistent, you are non-existent!*

In every other healthcare field, the client and the patient are one-in-the-same. Not in veterinary medicine, however. The patient experience and the client experience have to have their own systems. Let's see what Michael has to say about working with patients and clients.

CHAPTER

15

On the Subject of Patients and Clients

Michael E. Gerber

I don't build in order to have patients. I have patients in order to build.
—Ayn Rand

When it comes to the business of veterinary practice, the best definition of clients—in this case, the pet owners—I've ever heard is this:

Clients: *very special people who drive most veterinarians crazy.*

Does that work for you?

After all, it's a rare client who shows any appreciation for what a veterinarian has to go through to do the job as promised. Don't they always think the price is too high? And don't they focus on problems, broken promises, and the mistakes they think you make, rather than all the ways you bend over backward to give them what they need?

Do you ever hear other veterinarians voice these complaints? More to the point, have you ever voiced them yourself? Well, you're not alone. I have yet to meet a veterinarian who doesn't suffer from a strong case of client confusion.

Client confusion is about:

- what your client really wants;
- how to communicate effectively with your client;
- how to keep your client happy;
- how to deal with client dissatisfaction; and
- whom to call a client.

Confusion 1: What Your Client Really Wants

Your clients aren't just people; they're very specific kinds of people. Let me share with you the six categories of clients as seen from the E-Myth marketing perspective: (1) tactile clients, (2) neutral clients, (3) withdrawal clients, (4) experimental clients, (5) transitional clients, and (6) traditional clients.

Your entire marketing strategy must be based on which type of clients you are dealing with. Each of the six client types spends money on veterinary services for very different, and identifiable, reasons. These are:

- Tactile clients get their major gratification from interacting with other people.
- Neutral clients get their major gratification from interacting with inanimate objects (computers, cars, information).
- Withdrawal clients get their major gratification from interacting with ideas (thoughts, concepts, stories).
- Experimental clients rationalize their buying decisions by perceiving that what they bought is new, revolutionary, and innovative.
- Transitional clients rationalize their buying decisions by perceiving that what they bought is dependable and reliable.
- Traditional clients rationalize their buying decisions by perceiving that what they bought is cost-effective, a good deal, and worth the money.

In short:

- If your client is tactile, you have to emphasize the *people* of your practice.
- If your client is neutral, you have to emphasize the *technology* of your practice.
- If your client is a withdrawal patient, you have to emphasize the *idea* of your practice.
- If your client is experimental, you have to emphasize the *uniqueness* of your practice.
- If your client is transitional, you have to emphasize the *dependability* of your practice.
- If your client is traditional, you have to talk about the *financial competitiveness* of your practice.

What your clients want is determined by who they are. Who they are is regularly demonstrated by what they do. Think about the patients with whom you do business. Ask yourself: In which of the categories would I place them? What do they do for a living?

If your client is a mechanical engineer, for example, it's probably safe to assume he's a neutral client. If another one of your clients is a cardiologist, she's probably tactile. Accountants tend to be traditional, and software engineers are often experimental.

Having an idea about which categories your clients may fall into is very helpful to figuring out what they want. Of course, there's no exact science to it, and human beings constantly defy stereotypes. So don't take my word for it. You'll want to make your own analysis of the clients you serve.

Confusion 2: How to Communicate Effectively with Your Client

The next step in the client satisfaction process is to decide how to magnify the characteristics of your practice that are most likely to appeal to your preferred category of client. That begins with what marketing people call your positioning strategy.

What do I mean by positioning your practice? You position your practice with words. A few well-chosen words to tell your clients exactly what they want to hear. In marketing lingo, those words are called your unique selling proposition, or USP.

For example, if you are targeting tactile clients (ones who love people), your USP could be: "Weinstein Veterinary Hospital: where the feelings of people *really* count!"

If you are targeting experimental clients (ones who love new, revolutionary things), your USP could be: "Weinstein Veterinary Hospital: where living on the edge is a way of life!" In other words, when they choose to schedule an appointment with you, they can count on both your services and equipment to be on the cutting edge of the veterinary industry.

Is this starting to make sense? Do you see how the ordinary things most veterinarians do to get clients can be done in a significantly more effective way?

Once you understand the essential principles of marketing the E-Myth way, the strategies by which you attract clients can make an enormous difference in your market share.

Confusion 3: How to Keep Your Client Happy

Let's say you've overcome the first two confusions. Great. Now how do you keep your client happy?

Very simple: just keep your promises! And make sure your client *knows* you kept your promises every step of the way.

In short, giving your clients what they think they want is the key to keeping your clients (or anyone else, for that matter) really happy.

If your clients need to interact with people (high touch, tactile), make certain that they do.

If they need to interact with things (high-tech, neutral), make certain that they do.

If they need to interact with ideas (in their head, withdrawal), make certain that they do.

And so forth.

At E-Myth, we call this your *client fulfillment system*. It's the step-by-step process by which you do the task you've contracted to do and deliver what you've promised—on time, every time.

But what happens when your clients are not happy? What happens when you've done everything I've mentioned here and your client is still dissatisfied?

Confusion 4: How to Deal with Client Dissatisfaction

If you have followed each step up to this point, patient dissatisfaction will be rare. But it can and will still occur—people are people, and some people will always find a way to be dissatisfied with something. Here's what to do about it:

- Always listen to what your clients are saying. And never interrupt while they're saying it.
- After you're sure you've heard all of your client's complaint, make absolutely certain you understand what she said by phrasing a question, such as: "Can I repeat what you've just told me, Ms. Harton, to make absolutely certain I understand you?"
- Secure your client's acknowledgment that you have heard her complaint accurately.
- Apologize for whatever your client thinks you did that dissatisfied her—even if you didn't do it!
- After your client has acknowledged your apology, ask her exactly what would make her happy.
- Repeat what your client told you would make her happy, and get her acknowledgment that you have heard correctly.
- If at all possible, give your client exactly what she has asked for.

You may be thinking, "But what if my client wants something totally impossible?" Don't worry. If you've followed my recommendations to the letter, what your client asks for will seldom seem unreasonable.

Confusion 5: Whom to Call a Client

At this stage, it's important to ask yourself some questions about the kind of clients you hope to attract to your practice:

- Which types of clients would you most like to do business with?
- Where do you see your real market opportunities?
- Who would you like to work with, provide services to, and position your business for?

In short, *it's all up to you.* No mystery. No magic. Just a systematic process for shaping your practice's future. But you must have the passion to pursue the process. And you must be absolutely clear about every aspect of it.

Until you know your clients as well as you know yourself.

Until all your complaints about clients are a thing of the past.

Until you accept the undeniable fact that client acquisition and client satisfaction are more science than art.

But unless you're willing to grow your practice, you'd better not follow any of these recommendations. Because if you do what I'm suggesting, it's going to grow.

This brings us to the subject of *growth*. But first, let's see what Peter has to say about clients. ✤

CHAPTER

16

Clients Require Patience

Peter Weinstein, DVM, MBA

You can judge the morality of a nation by the way the society treats its animals.

—Mahatma Gandhi

Very early one morning I got a call from my staff that Sadie Landon was at the practice. Sadie was a black Labrador that we cared for. I was concerned that everything was okay since it was so early in the day. I inquired as to if everything was all right, and asked if I needed to get dressed and hurry in. Jennifer noted that everything was just fine and that Sadie was at the practice but Nancy, her mom, was not.

Sadie had walked out of her backyard, down the block, across a couple of busy intersections, and parked herself at the front door of the practice, waiting for us to let her in. And it wasn't even her normal bath day . . .

That is the first and last time that a patient voluntarily came in by themselves without the requisitely attached clients. In veterinary medicine, they (the patient and client) are routinely inseparable... and insufferable!

Converting from a doctor-centered practice to a client-centered practice requires a huge mindset shift. Most veterinarians went to veterinary school to take care of animals; the people are just in the way. Having been involved with the admissions process at a couple of veterinary schools, it is shocking how may prospective veterinarians truly love animals—large, small, feathered, scaled. And how many entered veterinary medicine because they really didn't want to deal with . . . *people!*

Every animal that we care for, from private practice to wildlife and everywhere in between, has a person who worries about them. The level of worry varies depending on the person.

The first thing I learned as a new veterinarian is that the client pays the bill. So client satisfaction and client services pay your salary. You need to learn about your clients as a person *and* their pet as a patient. The more you know about them, the more you will get to know about their animal friends.

When the entrepreneurial seizure hit and I opened my practice, I envisioned a Mayo Clinic–level of care in a Nordstrom-like service environment. Clinical needs and client service needs were put on equal levels. Easier said than done.

People needs—client service needs—are totally unpredictable from encounter to encounter, both between clients and within the same client at different times. And, although you can diagnose and treat virtually any animal disease, you are ill-prepared to diagnose and treat the individual needs and wants of the client whose pet you are caring for.

In spite of a focus on client service and people, based on our vision and our hiring, you still could never anticipate the client who could never be pleased. The practice was determined to give clients what they wanted at all times, if it all possible. We bent over backward, forward, sideways, and upside-down. And with the right people in place, we did pretty well.

The need for a systematic approach to client needs became apparent when we didn't have the right people on board after some long-term staff members moved on. With no systems in place, the new kids on the block were clueless at times. Their nametags, instead of reading "Professional Problem Solvers", should have read "We Make Things Worse". It became very apparent that you not only need the right people on board and the right systems on board, but you also need the right way to learn about your clients.

In contrast to other healthcare fields, where you are treating the patient and client concurrently, in veterinary practice, the patient's need could actually be greater than the client's ability to pay, or their interest in paying. In veterinary medicine—with no measurable impact of insurance; only some third-party payment options; and a human-animal bond that runs the gamut—you have to truly understand your clients better than they understand themselves. The psychographics and demographics primarily used for marketing purposes go a long way in determining the client relationship.

The para-professional staff at my practice was keyed in to patient needs and client needs. They learned to observe, to listen well, and to ask questions. The Welcome to the Practice Form became a great depository of client information that would help drive the client experience. Although I don't ever truly remember asking clients, "What is it you really want?" we were able to readily ascertain client needs while delivering on patient needs. Our focus on communication used various tools, from drawings and handwritten notes to computer-generated information sheets. We never hesitated to educate our clients, and maybe even went a little overboard when we communicated.

We had two goals in mind:

- Solve the client's and their pet's problems
- Keep them happy

The People System, or Controlling the Client Experience

From a consumer's standpoint, a customer's standpoint, you can never get it right. I like to think that the difference between a customer and a client is the second visit. If you have created a truly memorable experience for the customer, he or she will come back. And bring their friends. And spend more money. Your practice's goal is to get it right. What do you need to do to make the client happy so that he or she will approve the needed care for his or her animal?

The People System starts with your vision and primary aim. If service is not in your vision, it is hard to believe in it and even harder to deliver. After that, how well you deliver on that vision will determine your practice's position in the community.

You Get the Clients You Deserve

I remember working so hard to get new clients in our practice. Although we didn't have a formal acquisition marketing system at the beginning, we went out of our way to make every client happy. And our clients ran a wide gamut: Those whose pets were more important to them than children, and those whose pets simply served a utilitarian purpose. Those where the cost of care was never a barrier, and those where the cost of care was always the barrier. Those clients where you never could spend enough time with them, and those clients who were eager to get in and get out. Since we were trying to capture every possible client, we had to adjust our approach for every possible client. We didn't know about psychographics or demographics—we only knew that we needed clients.

When the client experience is so individualized, it is exhausting, chaotic, and has no measure of satisfaction *unless* the clients came back again and again and again. Eventually, after we found where to find the best clients for our practice *and* satisfy them and retain them, we could start to coordinate our healthcare delivery system and its associated processes. And then we could find the right staff members to help deliver on the promise that we made to the client—world-class care and world-class service.

Without a system in place, we got the clients we deserved. Those who drove us crazy, those who loved us, and those who were just kicking the tires looking for the best that they could afford. When we stopped trying to make everybody happy, we made everybody happy!

Making Clients Happy

We learned how to make clients happy by asking, listening, engaging, and caring. The staff worked on body language and communication skills, eye contact, and smiling. What did clients want? They wanted someone to listen to them, care about them and their pet, solve their problems, and do so in a way that they felt that they received value for their money. Our systems and processes did that.

The other thing we did was educate the clients about caring for their pets, what they could to at home, and what needed veterinary attention. We taught them what they needed to do to prevent problems and what they needed to do when they already had problems. Focusing on education was our unique selling proposition, and what we built our practice on. We were professional problem-solvers who under-promised and over-delivered when it came to communication and education. And we kept our promises.

We learned that it was all about *trust*. After many years of having services that were desperately needed turned down because of "the money," we realized that it was not, in fact, the money, but a lack of trust. Clients who second-guess the care you provide have not been given enough information and developed enough respect to trust you. This takes time and *must* be a focus for your staff.

With the ease of information on the Internet, Dr. Google, clients are more and more glutted with information, yet starved of knowledge. Your practice should have a Client Retention System that is knowledge-based; one where your practice is *the* source for pet healthcare. And an education-based system will help you get the follow-through that your patients need and the treatment that they deserve. People will gladly pay for knowledge and information—*and* your time!

One of the ways that we found out about the relationship of the pet in the household is by asking. On the Welcome to the Practice Form, there were three questions to help identify the patient-client relationship that, if answered honestly, helped us tremendously. Additionally, the entire staff was outstanding at listening and understanding client needs and wants. They knew that it wasn't just what clients said, but how they said it. Client-centricism was our practice's focus...but there were also the patients.

VPCR

The Veterinary-Patient-Client-Relationship: This is both a legal terminology from the practice act *and* a philosophical approach. In our opinion, you should always do:

- What is in the pet's best interest
- What is in the client's best interest
- What is in the staff's best interest
- What is in the doctor's best interest
- What is in the owner's best interest
- In that order (although pet and client may be held in parallel)

A patient-centered practice focuses on patient and client needs. When the client and patient are there, you must focus on their needs exclusively, and when they leave, they must remain in the front of your mind by continuing to help them understand how best to take care of their pets. Studies show that 70 percent of your clients will leave because of perceived indifference. Bottom line: you didn't care to care—when they were there *and* after they left.

A good friend of mine, an MD with a specialty in internal medicine, told me that his pediatrics rotation was nicknamed veterinary medicine. And it makes sense. In both fields, the parent and the pet owner are speaking on behalf of their child or pet. Both a parent and a pet owner are trying to help a sentient being remain healthy or become healthy; to get rid of disease or to get rid of pain. Communication using clear and concise words, interspersed metaphors and analogies (and a touch of humor) at an understandable level, and positive body language helps engender comfort and, most importantly, trust. It's about the patient, but it's also about the client.

Veterinary Medicine Would Be So Much Easier If It Weren't for the People

When you get together with a group of veterinarians for a dinner or a meeting or socially, this line is central to many discussions. Although it may feel true, it is not, in fact, the issue.

We need people to work with us as a part of our staff. We need people to care for the patients for whom we care. Veterinary medicine is a people-dependent, client-dependent, patient-dependent healthcare field. It is how we communicate, communicate, communicate that makes the people part so difficult.

So adjust your client focus to:

1. Know your clients better than they know themselves. How? Ask and listen.
2. Focus on creating a system to deliver to clients what they want in the manner that they want it, as if they were the *only* clients that you have.
3. Educate your clients to build their trust.
4. Under-promise and over-deliver with a client experience system.
5. It's about the ability to solve problems. Remember that.

With a client-centered practice delivering to your patients world-class care in a caring and compassionate way, you will start to achieve levels of success that you never imagined. If you have started to put the processes and systems together, you have built a foundation that is working. Until you start to grow and grow and grow. Are you ready for the growth? Michael will help you understand how to be prepared for the growth and what you need to do to survive it and thrive with it. ❖

CHAPTER

17

On the Subject of Growth

Michael E. Gerber

Growth is the only evidence of life.

—John Henry Newman, *Apologia Pro Vita Sua*

The rule of business growth says that every business, like every child, is destined to grow. Needs to grow. Is determined to grow.

Once you've created your veterinary practice, once you've shaped the idea of it, the most natural thing for it to do is to . . . *grow!* And if you stop it from growing, it will die.

Once a veterinarian has started a practice, it's his or her job to help it grow. To nurture it and support it in every way. To infuse it with

- Purpose;
- Passion;
- Will;

- Belief;
- Personality; and
- Method.

As your practice grows, it naturally changes. And as it changes from a small practice to something much bigger, you will begin to feel out of control. News flash: that's because you *are* out of control.

Your practice *has* exceeded your know-how, sprinted right past you, and now it's taunting you to keep up. That leaves you two choices: grow as big as your practice demands you grow, or try to hold your practice at its present level—at the level you feel most comfortable.

The sad fact is that most veterinarians do the latter. They try to keep their practice small, securely within their comfort zone. Doing what they know how to do, what they feel most comfortable doing. It's called playing it safe.

But as the practice grows, the number, scale, and complexity of tasks will grow, too, until they threaten to overwhelm the veterinarian. More people are needed. More space. More money. Everything seems to be happening at the same time. A hundred balls are in the air at once.

As I've said throughout this book: Most veterinarians are not entrepreneurs. They aren't true businesspeople at all, but technicians suffering from an entrepreneurial seizure. Their philosophy of coping with the workload can be summarized as "just do it," rather than figuring out how to get it done through other people using innovative systems to produce consistent results.

Given most veterinarians' inclination to be the master juggler in their practice, it's not surprising that as complexity increases, as work expands beyond their ability to do it, as money becomes more elusive, they are just holding on, desperately juggling more and more balls. In the end, most collapse under the strain.

You can't expect your practice to stand still. You can't expect your practice to stay small. A practice that stays small and depends on you to do everything isn't a practice—it's a job!

Yes, just like your children, your business must be allowed to grow, to flourish, to change, to become more than it is. In this way, it will match your vision. And you know all about vision, right? You'd better. It's what you do best!

Do you feel the excitement? You should. After all, you know what your practice is but not what it can be.

It's either going to grow or die. The choice is yours, but it is a choice that must be made. If you sit back and wait for change to overtake you, you will always have to answer no to this question: Are you ready?

This brings us to the subject of change. But first, let's see what Peter has to say about growth. ❖

CHAPTER

18

Growing Pains and Pleasures

Peter Weinstein, DVM, MBA

If you cannot risk, you cannot grow. If you cannot grow, you cannot become your best. If you cannot become your best, you cannot be happy. If you cannot be happy, what else matters?

—David Viscott, *Risk*

When you start something from scratch, there is only one direction you can go: *up!* However, it is sometimes hard to tell busyness from business. As a technician, I always felt busy doing it, doing it, doing it. As a manager, I made sure we were doing it the right way. As an entrepreneur, I saw busyness and business as one and the same and thought that was good.

As the practice grew and the chaos escalated, growth that was good became growth that was bad. Money was coming in, but the insanity was leading to more and more mistakes. We were growing but we didn't have the people or the systems in place to support the growth. Clients noticed the failures. Over-promising and under-delivering. Sending home the wrong pet with the wrong pet owner. Forgetting to send home leashes, collars, and prescriptions. Lab samples that were not picked up. Longer waiting times. Bathed animals going home dirty. Need I go on? I'm sure none of you ever had these issues!

The technician in me wanted to run away from the growth because I was losing control. The entrepreneur in me embraced the growth as great for accomplishing our long-term aim and vision. The manager . . . well, I think he developed multiple personality disorder just trying to make both other personalities happy.

Driving With One Foot on the Gas and the Other on the Brakes

After three years, we were at the same revenue level of many very well-established practices around us. But success is not just measured in dollars and cents, and after three strong years, the next year we plateaued and for the first time in our young life, the practice wasn't fun; neither was the business.

It was at this time that things started to get out of control. Being busier required adding more people, and without a system in place, there were mistakes made in the hiring process that led to people who just didn't fit the culture.

Being busier required more inventory, and that meant understanding what was turning over and what was burning up shelf space, and without a system in place, we sometimes over- or under-ordered, which was costly.

Clients complained or just never came back. Morale suffered, cohesiveness suffered, the staff started to break apart, and I learned that success wasn't all it was cracked up to be.

With the two biggest expenses not well managed, making more money (revenue) didn't mean we were making any more money (net). As much as making a lot of money was great, the stress associated with everything else started to wear on me, and all I wanted was to sell the practice and get out—after only three years! The technician in me was ready to run. The manager in me looked for help. And the entrepreneur wondered *why? Why* did I ever raise my hand for this job?

Hiring a veterinarian opened up some time to wear the manager's hat. Hiring a manager opened up some time to be the technician again. All at a financial cost to the practice and to me personally. There was no question in my mind that in order to get out of the malaise and to grow into the practice of my dreams, I had to get the practice under control. But what's a control freak to do?

It was around this time that the entrepreneur heard the famous words: *Work on your business and not just in your business!*

What Does That Mean?

Working in your business is easy. It is doing all the simple, menial tasks necessary to get through the day, the week, the month, the year. From being a clinician to being a toilet-paper-roll refill expert; from being a client service specialist to being a janitor; it is all about task management. Focus on the individual items that are done to get through the day just to exist.

Working on your business is hard. It means looking at everything that you do from a 35,000-foot perspective and asking, *why do we do it that way?* And if that is the best way, you continue to do it that way, and if not, you innovate and quantify it.

Working *in* your business is maintaining the status quo and being comfortable.

Working *on* your business means that status quo is not acceptable and that growth is the expectation.

But how do you know if you are growing or not?

The Glass Ceiling

Four years of veterinary school had me prepared to be a doctor. And if you just want to be a doctor, you will grow to a certain level of comfort and stay there. To be able to get over the hump, you need to get over the fear of business, managing, and growth.

There is a great scene in *Charlie and the Chocolate Factory* featuring Johnny Depp. After Charlie is chosen, he, Grandpa, and Mr. Wonka are in the glass elevator heading up.

Mr. Wonka: "*We're going to need to go much faster or we're never going to break through. I've been longing to push that button for years. Well, here we go! Up and out!*"

Grandpa: "*But it's made of glass! We'll smash into a million pieces!*"

So are you Grandpa or Mr. Wonka? Are you so concerned about growing your business that you'll never push the right buttons? Or are you eager to see whether the sky's the limit?

Before you push the button, however, you need to know where you are going (primary aim) and have the people and systems in place to get there. And you need to have some metrics that let you know that you are growing correctly.

Tic Marks on the Door Frame

As a kid growing up, did your mom or dad lean you up against the door frame every six months or every year and mark how tall you'd grown? These measurements were important to indicate your growth; some of your first benchmarks of success.

In your practice, what do you use as benchmarks of your practice's success? What are the key parameters that you monitor daily, weekly, monthly, and annually to measure your practice growth? You don't have any? Then how do you know that you're really growing?

Growth of your business is measurable. There are certain key performance indicators, like tic marks on the doorframe, that indicate how you're doing. If you are not monitoring these areas, you are flying blindly.

Some commonly tracked KPIs/Key Performance Indicators include:

- Number of transactions
- Average client transaction
- Daily, monthly revenue
- Monthly, annual expenses
- Number of new clients
- Appointment-book fill
- Number of surgeries
- Number of dentistries

And the list goes on.

What are your success parameters or metrics? How often do you monitor them? Does your staff know what you need to do on a daily, weekly, or monthly basis to meet your goals for success? If they don't know, how can they help you become successful?

Open-Book Management

Ever since Dr. Ross Clark suggested Open-Book Management (OBM) for veterinary hospitals twenty-five years ago, it has been a controversial topic. For some reason, veterinarians, and in some cases their staffs, are loath to knowing what's going on. And they are even less likely to share this information with those around them who can actually influence the numbers.

In my practice, we shared some select numbers with the staff, those numbers that they could truly influence. The number of transactions, for example, is completely impacted by the systems that you have in place for booking appointments, scheduling re-checks, marketing to new clients, and marketing to existing clients. And who is in charge of those systems? (Please don't say the owner or doctor. If you did, go back to chapter one and start over.) The *staff*.

Tracking and sharing numbers with your staff so that they can influence the practice, and more importantly so that they can share in the success of the practice financially, is very effective. Your staff should know what to do when numbers are out of whack, and they should be celebrated when they are growing. Staff-based healthcare shares in the pain and the pleasure, and the systems that deliver it are set up for guaranteed success.

Growth Removal

What if you stopped growing? What would happen? The first thing you would feel is the change in cash flow. The expenses wouldn't change, but the income would. There would be too much month left at the end of the money. And when that happens, you aren't going to stop paying yourself, so somebody(ies) have to go. And then:

- Staff get laid off and morale goes down.
- Upgrades for technology, software, and hardware are delayed, and things stop working.
- With fewer staff and technology failures, what you delegated before goes away and you return to doing it, doing it, doing it. The technician thrives while the entrepreneur cries.
- The lack of technology impacts the quality of care, and the patients and clients both suffer.
- Upkeep on the facility is put off and cracks get bigger; stains get larger; odors become more prevalent; and everything looks older.
- And bonuses . . . *fuhgedaboutit*.

So learning to manage the benefits of growth, while planning for the complications of growth, must be a part of your plan for success. Remember, it's all about the systems, people, and profit!

Would you tell your kids to stop growing? A fear of success makes no sense to me. Why wouldn't you want your practice to grow? Since when does having more time and making more money carry negative connotations?

But you want growth that is in control. The processes-and-systems mentality allows you to grow financially while staying in control from a business, management, and personal standpoint.

Your practice is a living, breathing organism just like you and your kids. Feed it the right food, mix in exercise, throw in a dash of education, and a handful of rules and policies, and stir.

In practice terms:

1. Never stop learning about your practice and never stop working on your practice, even when you stop working in your practice as much.
2. Learn what metrics tell you how you're doing. Whether it is sit-ups or pushups or the number of bench press reps you do, you have measurements for your physical fitness. What is your practice target for success in your business?
3. Work on the processes and systems that you need to get in control. If you work out but you don't use the right technique, you can hurt your back or neck or legs. If you run your business without the right techniques, systems, processes, or recipes, you run the risk of hurting the economic health of the business. Learn to do it the right way.
4. Learn to delegate and release while holding on to leadership. If you want your kids to walk, you have to encourage them to walk, which doesn't mean picking them up when they fall and holding them. It means helping them to get up and try again. Just like you let your kids grow by trial and error within safe guidelines, let your staff do the same. Grow from your mistakes while learning how not to make them again.

Growth is scary, invigorating, challenging, and an absolute necessity for turning your practice into a business, and subsequently an enterprise, in the long term. Growth doesn't come without change. In fact, they could be considered codependent. Let's see what Michael has to say about change, a truly foundational term in this discussion. ✤

CHAPTER

19

On the Subject of Change

Michael E. Gerber

There is nothing permanent except change.
—Heraclitus of Ephesus, *Lives of the Philosophers*

So your practice is growing. That means, of course, that it's also changing. Which means it's driving you and everyone in your life crazy.

That's because, to most people, change is a diabolical thing. Tell most people they have to change, and their first instinct is to crawl into a hole. Nothing threatens their existence more than change. Nothing cements their resistance more than change. Nothing.

Yet for the past thirty-five years, that's exactly what I've been proposing to small-business owners: the need to change. Not for the sake of change itself, but for the sake of their lives.

I've talked to countless veterinarians whose hopes weren't being realized through their practice; whose lives were consumed by work; who slaved increasingly longer hours for decreasing pay; whose dissatisfaction grew as their enjoyment shriveled; whose practice had become the worst job in the world; whose money was out of control; whose employees were a source of never-ending hassles—just like their patients, their bank, and, increasingly, even their families.

More and more, these veterinarians spent their time alone, dreading the unknown and anxious about the future. And even when they were with people, they didn't know how to relax. Their mind was always on the job. They were distracted by work, by the thought of work. By the fear of falling behind.

And yet, when confronted with their condition and offered an alternative, most of the same veterinarians strenuously resisted. They assumed that if there were a better way of doing business, they already would have figured it out. They derived comfort from knowing what they believed they already knew. They accepted the limitations of being a veterinarian; or the truth about people; or the limitations of what they could expect from their patients, their employees, their staff members, their bankers—even their family and friends.

In short, most veterinarians I've met over the years would rather live with the frustrations they already have than risk enduring new frustrations.

Isn't that true of most people you know? Rather than opening up to the infinite number of possibilities life offers, they prefer to shut their life down to respectable limits. After all, isn't that the most reasonable way to live?

I think not. I think we must learn to let go. I think that if you fail to embrace change, it will inevitably destroy you.

Conversely, by opening yourself to change, you give your veterinary practice the opportunity to get the most from your talents.

Let me share with you an original way to think about change, about life, about who we are and what we do. About the stunning notion of expansion and contraction.

Contraction vs. Expansion

"Our salvation," a wise man once said, "is to allow." That is, to be open, to let go of our beliefs, to change. Only then can we move from a point of view to a viewing point.

That wise man was Thaddeus Golas, the author of a small, powerful book entitled *The Lazy Man's Guide to Enlightenment* (Seed Center, 1971).

Among the many inspirational things he had to say was this compelling idea:

> *The basic function of each being is expanding and contracting. Expanded beings are permeative; contracted beings are dense and impermeative. Therefore each of us, alone or in combination, may appear as space, energy, or mass, depending on the ratio of expansion to contraction chosen, and what kind of vibrations each of us expresses by alternating expansion and contraction. Each being controls his own vibrations.*

In other words, Golas tells us that the entire mystery of life can be summed up in two words: *expansion* and *contraction*. He goes on to say:

> *We experience expansion as awareness, comprehension, understanding, or whatever we wish to call it.*
>
> *When we are completely expanded, we have a feeling of total awareness, of being one with all life.*
>
> *At that level we have no resistance to any vibrations or interactions of other beings. It is timeless bliss, with unlimited choice of consciousness, perception, and feeling.*
>
> *When a [human] being is totally contracted, he is a mass particle, completely imploded.*
>
> *To the degree that he is contracted, a being is unable to be in the same space with others, so contraction is felt as fear, pain, unconsciousness, ignorance, hatred, evil, and a whole host of strange feelings.*
>
> *At an extreme [of contraction, a human being] has the feeling of being completely insane, of resisting everyone and everything, of being unable to choose the content of his consciousness.*

> *Of course, these are just the feelings appropriate to mass vibration levels, and he can get out of them at any time by expanding, by letting go of all resistance to what he thinks, sees, or feels.*

Stay with me here. Because what Golas says is profoundly important. When you're feeling oppressed, overwhelmed, exhausted by more than you can control—contracted, as Golas puts it—you can change your state to one of expansion.

According to Golas, the more contracted we are, the more threatened by change; the more expanded we are, the more open to change.

In our most enlightened—that is, open—state, change is as welcome as non-change. Everything is perceived as a part of ourselves. There is no inside or outside. Everything is one thing. Our sense of isolation is transformed to a feeling of ease, of light, of joyful relationship with everything.

As infants, we didn't even think of change in the same way, because we lived those first days in an unthreatened state. Insensitive to the threat of loss, most young children are only aware of *what is*. Change is simply another form of *what is*. Change just *is*.

However, when we are in our most contracted—that is, closed—state, change is the most extreme threat. If the known is what I have, then the unknown must be what threatens to take away what I have. Change, then, is the unknown. And the unknown is fear. It's like being between trapezes.

- To the fearful, change is threatening because things may get worse.
- To the hopeful, change is encouraging because things may get better.
- To the confident, change is inspiring because the challenge exists to improve things.

If you are fearful, you see difficulties in every opportunity. If you are fear-free, you see opportunities in every difficulty.

Fear protects what I have from being taken away. But it also disconnects me from the rest of the world. In other words, fear keeps me separate and alone.

Here's the exciting part of Golas's message: with this new understanding of contraction and expansion, we can become completely attuned to where we are at all times.

If I am afraid, suspicious, skeptical, and resistant, I am in a contracted state. If I am joyful, open, interested, and willing, I am in an expanded state. Just knowing this puts me on an expanded path. Always remembering this, Golas says, brings enlightenment, which opens me even more.

Such openness gives me the ability to freely access my options. And taking advantage of options is the best part of change. Just as there are infinite ways to greet a client, there are infinite ways to run your company. If you believe Thaddeus Golas, your most exciting option is to be open to all of them.

Because your life is lived on a continuum between the most contracted and most expanded—the most closed and most open—states, change is best understood as the movement from one to the other, and back again.

Most small-business owners I've met see change as a thing in itself, as something that just happens to them. Most experience change as a threat. Whenever change shows up at the door, they quickly slam it. Many bolt the door and pile up the furniture. Some even run for their gun.

Few of them understand that change isn't a thing in itself, but rather the manifestation of many things. You might call it the revelation of all possibilities. Think of it as the ability at any moment to sacrifice what we are for what we could become.

Change can either challenge us or threaten us. It's our choice. Our attitude toward change can either pave the way to success or throw up a roadblock.

Change is where opportunity lives. Without change we would stay exactly as we are. The universe would be frozen still. Time would end.

At any given moment, we are somewhere on the path between a contracted and expanded state. Most of us are in the middle of the journey, neither totally closed nor totally open. According to Golas, change is our movement from one place in the middle toward one of the two ends.

Do you want to move toward contraction or toward enlightenment? Because without change, you are hopelessly stuck with what you've got.

Without change,

- we have no hope;
- we cannot know true joy;
- we will not get better; and
- we will continue to focus exclusively on what we have and the threat of losing it.

All of this negativity contracts us even more, until, at the extreme closed end of the spectrum, we become a black hole so dense that no light can get in or out.

Sadly, the harder we try to hold on to what we've got, the less able we are to do so. So we try still harder, which eventually drags us even deeper into the black hole of contraction.

Are you like that? Do you know anybody who is?

Think of change as the movement between where we are and where we're not. That leaves only two directions for change: either moving forward or slipping backward. We become either more contracted or more expanded.

The next step is to link change to how we feel. If we feel afraid, change is dragging us backward. If we feel open, change is pushing us forward.

Change is not a thing in itself, but a movement of our consciousness. By tuning in, by paying attention, we get clues to the state of our being.

Change, then, is not an outcome or something to be acquired. Change is a shift of our consciousness, of our being, of our humanity, of our attention, of our relationship with all other beings in the universe.

We are either "more in relationship" or "less in relationship." Change is the movement in either of those directions. The exciting part is that *we possess the ability to decide which way we go . . . and to know, in the moment, which way we're moving.*

Closed, open . . . Open, closed. Two directions in the universe. The choice is yours.

Do you see the profound opportunity available to you? What an extraordinary way to live!

Enlightenment is not reserved for the sainted. Rather, it comes to us as we become more sensitive to ourselves. Eventually, we become our own guides, alerting ourselves to our state, moment by moment: *open . . . closed . . . open . . . closed.*

Listen to your inner voice, your ally, and feel what it's like to be open and closed. Experience the instant of choice in both directions.

You will feel the awareness growing. It may be only a flash at first, so be alert. This feeling is accessible, but only if you avoid the black hole of contraction.

Are you afraid that you're totally contracted? Don't be—it's doubtful. The fact that you're still reading this book suggests that you're moving in the opposite direction.

You're more like a running back seeking the open field. You can see the opportunity gleaming in the distance. In the open direction.

Understand that I'm not saying that change itself is a point on the path; rather, it's the all-important movement.

Change is *in you*, not *out there*.

What path are you on? The path of liberation? Or the path of crystallization?

As we know, change can be for the better or for the worse.

If change is happening *inside* of you, it is for the worse only if you remain closed to it. The key, then, is your attitude—your acceptance or rejection of change. Change can be for the better only if you accept it. And it will certainly be for the worse if you don't.

Remember, change is nothing in itself. Without you, change doesn't exist. Change is happening inside of each of us, giving us clues to where we are at any point in time.

Rejoice in change, for it's a sign you are alive.

Are we open? Are we closed? If we're open, good things are bound to happen. If we're closed, things will only get worse.

According to Golas, it's as simple as that. Whatever happens defines where we are. *How* we are is *where* we are. It cannot be any other way.

For change is life.

Charles Darwin wrote, "It is not the strongest of the species that survive, nor the most intelligent, but the one that proves itself most responsive to change."

The growth of your veterinary practice, then, is its change. Your role is to go with it, to be with it, to share the joy, embrace the opportunities, meet the challenges, and learn the lessons.

Remember, there are three kinds of people: (1) those who make things happen, (2) those who let things happen, and (3) those who wonder what the hell happened. The people who make things happen are masters of change. The other two are its victims.

Which type are you?

The Big Change

If all this is going to mean anything to the life of your practice, you have to know when you're going to leave it. At what point, in your practice's rise from where it is now to where it can ultimately grow, are you going to sell it? Because if you don't have a clear picture of when you want out, your practice is the master of your destiny, not the reverse.

As we stated earlier, the most valuable form of money is equity, and unless your business vision includes your equity and how you will use it to your advantage, you will forever be consumed by your practice.

Your practice is potentially the best friend you ever had. It is your practice's nature to serve you, so let it. If, however, you are not a wise steward, if you do not tell your practice what you expect from it, it will run rampant, abuse you, use you, and confuse you.

Change. Growth. Equity.

Focus on the point in the future when you will take leave of your practice. Now reconsider your goals in that context. Be specific. Write them down.

Skipping this step is like tiptoeing through earthquake country. Who can say where the fault lies waiting? And who knows exactly when your whole world may come crashing down around you?

Which brings us to the subject of *time*. But first, let's see what Peter has to say about change. ✦

CHAPTER

20

Time for a Change

Peter Weinstein, DVM, MBA

The responsibility for change, therefore, lies with us. We must begin with ourselves, teaching ourselves not to close our minds prematurely to the novel, the surprising, the seemingly radical. This means fighting off the idea-assassins who rush forward to kill any new suggestion on grounds of its impracticality, while defending whatever now exists as practical, no matter how absurd, oppressive, or unworkable it may be.

—Alvin Toffler, *The Third Wave*

If your practice and life are perfect and what you want them to be, you can skip to the next chapter; this discussion isn't for you. Unless, of course, you think that they could be better!

In looking to fuse Michael's discussion on change with my own thoughts on the topic, I realized that the technician in me keeps looking at change differently from the manager and the entrepreneur. Defined by *Merriam-Webster Dictionary*, the active verb *change* means, "to make different in some particular." However, there are more passive verb definitions—"to become different"—and noun definitions—"the act, process, or result of changing."

As a business owner, the entrepreneur, I saw change as the only way to get closer to my primary aim. Status quo is like a sailboat in a dead calm. Quiet. Unmoving. But not exactly safe. Ultimate success required a tailwind that moved you forward in a controlled fashion. The entrepreneur set the sails and changed the course to get closer and closer to the final destination in the most effective, efficient, and profitable manner.

As the manager, my role was to navigate the course set by the entrepreneur. I kept the ship on course and directed the changes needed to attain the primary aim.

The technician . . . well, the technician's role is just to do what is asked. And in most cases, the technician doesn't initiate change but is asked to change to meet the greater needs of the business. The technician, in most cases, is the one most resistant to change. And that is the comfort zone that most veterinarians find themselves in. The technician hat is solidly in place, and please don't try to remove it.

It took me about three years, as mentioned, to learn that a technician-driven business does not change. We were very good at doing the tasks necessary to deliver the services, vaccines, spays, neuters, baths, dental cleanings, lump removals, itchy skin exams, vomiting cat exams, diarrhea exams to a clientele who was satisfied with the service that they received. But to me, satisfied wasn't enough. Extremely satisfied, raving fans was the ultimate desire. However, the technician in me really didn't want to rock the boat—until the entrepreneur realized the boat wasn't moving!

Answer: The Depth

Question: "What's the difference between a rut and a grave?"

Do you remember the movie *Groundhog Day?* Bill Murray plays Phil Connors, an arrogant and egocentric Pittsburgh TV weatherman who, during an assignment covering the annual Groundhog

Day event in Punxsutawney, Pennsylvania, finds himself in a time loop, repeating the same day again and again.

For years, my alarm was set at the same time. I would get out of bed and follow the same morning routine. Leave the house at the same time every day and take the same route to work. I was programmed and it felt comfortable because I didn't have to think about it. And then road construction began and my exit was closed for four months. Then the road construction moved and my on-ramp was closed for three months. Do you know how hard it was to reprogram myself? I was in a rut. And so was my practice.

What's a technician to do? Call the manager? I don't think so! They manage change; they don't envision change. Call the entrepreneur? Absolutely! This entrepreneur realized that small changes weren't the answer; radical changes were needed. There are few things in life more stressful than starting up a business. One of these is moving your business from its comfortable location to a new location, and trying to conduct business while doing so. But that is what we did. And it shook up the malaise.

The new location required some new systems, which we developed and introduced. The new location required some new staff, whom we hired using some different approaches, and it worked. The new location worked because we worked *on* it before we worked *in* it.

The impact of the change was felt financially. But more importantly, the staff felt it. They saw that the leadership had a vision and a drive to improve the practice and the practice environment for the staff, the patients, and the clients.

We had changed the practice, but we had also changed the way we thought.

Fear Factor

In an article by Harvey Mackay entitled, "Be Open to Change or Be Left Behind," he writes: "A Canadian neurosurgeon made some dramatic discoveries when he was researching the human mind's reaction to change. His experiments proved that when a person is forced to change a fundamental belief or opinion, the brain undergoes a series of nervous sensations equivalent to distressing torture."

Ever have one of these déjà vu experiences?

Did you have the grandparents who had plastic covers on the living room furniture? It wasn't that long ago that I walked into a veterinarian's office and immediately went back in time to the first practice I worked in the '70s: wood-panel walls; wrinkled, faded staff scrubs; dust under the chairs; posters taped to the walls; orange Formica; cracked tile floors; disinfectant smell; chain-link runs. Going back in time told me what this owner thought of change.

What was interesting was that in the midst of this Vietnam War–era décor, the practice had all of the new technologies: digital dental radiology; digital radiography; ultrasound; paperless practice.

So the technician got his toys, but the entrepreneur obviously wasn't engaged. Veterinarians readily accept technology changes, but they don't always think about the financial, operational, process, or systems changes required to add new technology, nor does it seem to cause them the pain that a remodel or move might cause. Interesting!

To the hospital staff in the above-mentioned practice, the addition of technology did nothing for the chaos, nor did it change the poverty and scarcity mentality of the owner. Rather than investing in the needed changes that would have improved the practice environment, the technician won the battle, while the entrepreneur and manager were losing the war. The fear of change in practice operations and systems is obviously greater than the fear of spending money in this practice. Torture!

Change Your Mind

Moore's Law says that the processing power of computers will double every two years. It is also reported that healthcare knowledge doubles every two years.

The veterinary profession as a whole, from organized veterinary medicine to the practice level, is thought to be glacial in its willingness to change. The inertia of decades of doing it the same way has created a resistance to looking in the windshield and continuing to focus on the rearview mirror.

In case you disagree with the above:

- How did you feel when the discussion of changing vaccination schedules from an annual to an every-three-year program was going on?
- How about the integration of pre-anesthetic blood work into your surgical protocols?
- And pain management?
- And more recently, the change of Tramadol into a scheduled substance?
- I can't tell you how much griping, complaining, grumbling, and protesting that I heard. Were you one of the whiners or one of the winners?

I've heard it all or I've said it myself: *I can't afford to change. Change won't help. It works; why change? I don't know how to change.*

Time to get out of your rut. Embrace change. Change is an ally.

Not change for the sake of change, nor just to be disruptive, but change to strategically position your practice in your community. It won't be comfortable, but it is required to avoid the obscurity in which you currently labor. Trust me, it won't be as painful as torture. The decision to change is *slooooooow*; the impact of change is instantaneous.

And it can be pleasurable. Financially, as well as psychologically.

What would happen if...

- You took a different route to work?
- You bought some scrubs for your staff (and let them choose the ones they want)?

- You tried doing surgery from the other side of the table (torture!)?
- You added an online pharmacy?
- You decided to go to paperless medical records?
- You implemented an exam room and transcription assistant?
- You took a day to work *on* your practice and not *in* your practice?

It is time to look at things differently. What got you here won't get you there (apologies to Marshall Goldsmith).

If you really want to get started on change, you need to know where you are going. What is your vision, your primary aim? What will your practice look like if it were to deliver the perfect experience for clients and patients? Write it down.

Next, where are you now relative to where you want to be? The entrepreneur and manager need to start being present in your practice. No more falling asleep at the wheel. Look at the way patients and clients flow through the practice. Observe client service operations, from the phone through the collection of payments. Sit in the lobby while life happens. How is inventory mismanaged? Does the physical plant, as it looks now, deliver on your vision? Are you fulfilling your clients and patients needs? How can you improve your efficiency? Your effectiveness? Your value proposition? Your unique selling proposition? Work your way from the 35,000-foot level to the molecular in reviewing your practice. How are your systems, if any, working?

With the evidence collected, it is time to create the processes and systems that will change your practice. And with them, the results that you will get.

A2 = G2

The first time I saw this equation from Dr. Tom Catanzaro, I thought it was either a calculus formula or some micro-economics theorem. It is neither. Here is the solution to the formula:

If you Always do what you've Always done,
you'll always Get what you've always Got.

Change is not a choice. Change happens. You can accept it or resist it; resistance is futile.

Jack Welch said, "Do you have the ability and self-confidence to take chances, to reach, to probe, and the self awareness to know what you don't know?"

You need to take charge of change if you want to get different results. Don't tell me you don't have time to change. You don't have time *not* to change. It's time for Michael to discuss time as it applies to your practice, business, and eventual enterprise. ✤

CHAPTER

21

On the Subject of Time

Michael E. Gerber

Take time to deliberate; but when the time for action arrives, stop thinking and go in.

—Andrew Jackson

"I'm running out of time!" veterinarians often lament. "I have to learn how to manage my time more carefully!"

Of course, they see no real solution to this problem. They're just worrying the subject to death. Singing the veterinarian's blues.

Some make a real effort to control time. Maybe they go to time-management classes, or faithfully try to record their activities during every hour of the day.

But it's hopeless. Even when veterinarians work harder, even when they keep precise records of their time, there's always a shortage of it. It's as if they're looking at a square clock in a round universe. Something doesn't fit. The result: the veterinarian is constantly chasing work, money, life.

And the reason is simple. Veterinarians don't see time for what it really is. They think of time with a small "t," rather than Time with a capital "T."

Yet Time is simply another word for your *life*. It's your ultimate asset, your gift at birth—and you can spend it any way you want. Do you know how you want to spend it? Do you have a plan?

How do *you* deal with Time? Are you even conscious of it? If you are, I bet you are constantly locked into either the future or the past. Relying on either memory or imagination.

Do you recognize these voices? "Once I get through this, I can have a drink . . . go on a vacation . . . retire." "I remember when I was young and practicing veterinary medicine was satisfying."

As you go to bed at midnight, are you thinking about waking up at 7 a.m. so that you can get to the office by 8 a.m. so that you can go to lunch by noon, because your software people will be there at 1:30 p.m. and you have a full schedule and a new patient scheduled for 2:30 p.m.?

Most of us are prisoners of the future or the past. While pinballing between the two, we miss the richest moments of our life—the present. Trapped forever in memory or imagination, we are strangers to the here and now. Our future is nothing more than an extension of our past, and the present is merely the background.

It's sobering to think that right now each of us is at a precise spot somewhere between the beginning of our Time (our birth) and the end of our Time (our death). No wonder everyone frets about Time. What really terrifies us is that *we're using up our life and we can't stop it*.

It feels as if we're plummeting toward the end with nothing to break our free fall. Time is out of control! Understandably, this is horrifying, mostly because the real issue is not time with a small "t" but Death with a big "D."

From the depths of our existential anxiety, we try to put Time in a different perspective—all the while pretending we can manage it. We talk about Time as though it were something other than what it is. "Time is money," we announce, as though that explains it.

But what every veterinarian should know is that Time is life. And Time ends! Life ends!

The big, walloping, irresolvable problem is that *we don't know how much Time we have left*.

Do you feel the fear? Do you want to get over it?

Let's look at Time more seriously.

To fully grasp Time with a capital "T," you have to ask the big Question: *How do I wish to spend the rest of my Time?*

Because I can assure you that if you don't ask that big Question with a big "Q," you will forever be assailed by the little questions. You'll shrink the whole of your life to *this time* and *next time* and the *last time*—all the while wondering, *what time is it?*

It's like running around the deck of a sinking ship worrying about where you left the keys to your cabin.

You must accept that you have only so much Time; that you're using up that Time second by precious second. And that your Time, your life, is the most valuable asset you have. Of course, you can use your Time any way you want. But unless you choose to use it as richly, as rewardingly, as excitingly, as intelligently, as *intentionally* as possible, you'll squander it and fail to appreciate it.

Indeed, if you are oblivious to the value of your Time, you'll commit the single greatest sin: You will live your life unconscious of its passing you by.

Until you deal with Time with a capital "T," you'll worry about time with a small "t" until you have no Time—or life—left. Then your Time will be history . . . along with your life.

I can anticipate the question: If Time is the problem, why not just take on fewer patients? Well, that's certainly an option, but probably not necessary. I know a veterinarian with a small practice who sees four times as many patients as the average, yet the he and his staff don't work long hours. How is it possible?

This veterinarian has a system. By using this expert system, the employees can do everything the veterinarian or his staff members would do—everything that isn't veterinarian-dependent.

Be Versus Do

Remember when we all asked, "What do I want to be when I grow up?" It was one of our biggest concerns as children.

Notice that the question isn't, "What do I want to *do* when I grow up?" It's "What do I want to *be?*"

Shakespeare wrote, "To be or not to be." Not "To do or not to do."

But when you grow up, people always ask you, "What do you *do?*" How did the question change from *being* to *doing?* How did we miss the critical distinction between the two?

Even as children, we sensed the distinction. The real question we were asking was not what we would end up *doing* when we grew up, but who we would *be*.

We were talking about a *life* choice, not a *work* choice. We instinctively saw it as a matter of how we spend our Time, not what we do in time.

Look to children for guidance. I believe that as children we instinctively saw Time as life and tried to use it wisely. As children, we wanted to make a life choice, not a work choice. As children, we didn't know—or care—that work had to be done on time, on budget.

Until you see Time for what it really is—your life span—you will always ask the wrong question.

Until you embrace the whole of your Time and shape it accordingly, you will never be able to fully appreciate the moment.

Until you fully appreciate every second that comprises Time, you will never be sufficiently motivated to live those seconds fully.

Until you're sufficiently motivated to live those seconds fully, you will never see fit to change the way you are. You will never take the quality and sanctity of Time seriously.

And unless you take the sanctity of Time seriously, you will continue to struggle to catch up with something behind you. Your frustrations will mount as you try to snatch the second that just whisked by.

If you constantly fret about time with a small "t," then Time will blow right past you. And you'll miss the whole point, the real truth about Time: You can't manage it; you never could. You can only live it.

And so that leaves you with these questions: How do I live my life? How do I give significance to it? How can I be here now, in this moment?

Once you begin to ask these questions, you'll find yourself moving toward a much fuller, richer life. But if you continue to be caught up in the banal work you do every day, you're never going to find the time to take a deep breath, exhale, and be present in the now.

So, let's talk about the subject of *work*. But first, let's find out what Peter has to say about time. ✦

CHAPTER

22

Just Killing Time

Peter Weinstein, DVM, MBA

Either you run the day or the day runs you.

—Jim Rohn

Birthing a practice and a baby . . . there isn't much difference. Sleep deprivation runs rampant and you can never recover the lost sleep. They both require a lot of attention for reasons you just don't understand. There are a lot of books on child rearing and entrepreneurship, but neither prepares you for the experience. You can feed it, clean it, care for it, and love it and neither will stop asking for more...money, energy, and time.

As a young business owner, I knew that I had bitten off a huge time commitment, but I always thought I would be able to reel it in and keep control of it. However, as we got busier, we didn't become more efficient. Instead, the busier we got, the more time I dedicated to the clients and the less time I gave myself.

As has been the theme throughout this book, business control, and subsequently self-control, didn't come until I understood systems and working on the business more than *in* it.

As a parent you aim to raise your kids to make good decisions and to be successful on their own. As a business owner, your aim should be to raise your business through good decisions so that it can be successful on its own. If you spend too much time doing for your kids, they may not be able to succeed on their own. If you spend too much time doing for your business, not only is their no guarantee that your business will be successful, but you won't be there to raise your kids either.

Your Time, Your Life

Michael's philosophical outlook on time assigns two types: the little 't' of time spent at work and the big 'T' of time spent on life. So often, when I was in practice, the two ts were so intertwined that they were inseparable.

I could never leave the practice even after I left the practice. I was thinking about case outcomes, staff attitude issues, a burgeoning inventory, physical plant problems, sales tax reports, and the list continued. I would go to sleep thinking of one challenge and wake up thinking of another. Separating the two ts was impossible. And it was impacting the big T, my personal time inexorably. When your big T is impacted, you don't look forward to your little t. Work became a time leech sucking away minutes of big T to fill the need of the little-t leech.

If you haven't thought about it, think about it. How we use our little-t time impacts our big-T time.

Little-T Time (Work-Associated Time)

- You arrive at work late; you are already behind.
- You leave early to get to work; you subtract from family time.
- An appointment shows up late and the rest of day's time shifts

(unless you have systems in place to handle this) so you won't get home on time.

- An emergency shows up at the end of the day; there goes a hot dinner and kid time.
- You have a meeting at night; there goes family time.
- You have a wedding you must attend; there goes income-producing time at work.
- The littlest kid is in the school concert at lunch; there goes client time.
- You can't get back family time by leaving work early—this isn't a bank.
- You can't get back work hours by staying late—this isn't a bank.

Big-T Time (Your Life Time)

Wrapping your arms around this concept means understanding the importance of relationships that are business in nature. It means not feeling guilty about having fun when you could be working. It means slowing down and smelling the roses (thank you, Dr. Joe Cortese).

In recent years, too many of my colleagues have been taken way too young. It makes you realize that you have to stop and smell the roses. You have to find *time* for your family and friends because you never know when . . .

Controlling *time* means taking action sooner rather than later. Making mistakes by taking chances is better than wasting time trying to decide what to do. It is not ready-aim-go with the emphasis on *aim*. It is ready, go with the emphasis on go. Taking aim takes time, and as we've discussed, time just disappears way too quickly.

It means prioritizing your time to ensure you have more *time*.

24/7/365

Time is an interesting discussion. I frequently think of time as a finite dimension. We are only given so much of it. How you take that value, whatever it is, and distribute it around determines a great deal of your happiness and success.

As an associate veterinarian or as and owner wearing a technician's title, your time is spent doing tasks for which you are given a paycheck. Work an hour, get paid for an hour's work. Essentially, you can only make so much because there are only so many hours in a day, week, month, year, lifetime.

You can buy love, buy money, buy health…the one thing you can't buy is time. Or can you?

Time and Success

Here are a few simple things you can learn to do.

Leverage: In looking at colleagues and at my practice, freeing up time came from building a staff that stays together and plays together and that I had trained to a level of trust so that I could focus on my most productive tasks and delegate anything and everything else.

By learning to leverage your time and focus, your energy is on high-return actions; while letting others focus on lower-return actions, you are essentially buying time.

Think about it . . .

- Seeing clients in an exam room = $200/hour
- Putting in an IV catheter = $18/hour
- Negotiating to purchase a property for a larger facility= Priceless

If you are in an exam room seeing clients while somebody else is putting in that catheter, you are buying time by having somebody handling that task. If you can put somebody into the exam room and generate income while you are thinking big picture . . . well, that is a great return on your time, isn't it?

Self Control: As a technician you do tasks in exchange for time; as an entrepreneur you control your time and dedicate it to your most productive performances. You have to control where your energy goes. If you do not dedicate your time to peak performance, you end up with the ongoing drudgery of taskmastering. Thus, control yourself and you can control your time. You don't manage time. Time-management courses are a waste of time. You manage yourself and what you do with your time.

Scheduling Your Time

As a business owner, you are trying to balance the three balls of technician, manager, and entrepreneur. In my experience, if you try to do this concurrently, you will find yourself with more balls in the air than a one-handed cat neuterer (inside veterinary joke). You must set aside minutes or hours of each day that are dedicated strictly to wearing each of the above-mentioned hats.

As I grew in my practice and added professional and management help, I dedicated either days or half-days to the management role with no clinical responsibilities. These management days were just that, management days—no clinical responsibilities. The clinical days were just that, clinical days. And, as in most cases, the entrepreneur days were few and far between, but they definitely required time away from the practice. Time to think, visualize, and dream about the future.

As a single doctor business owner, you must schedule time off the books to manage and visualize; you cannot do it between appointments. Managing between appointments gives you no time to gather information and make knowledgeable decisions. You will micromanage and emotionally manage issues that are not supposed to be knee-jerk-managed.

It is perfectly fine to block off management time and entrepreneur time. In fact, it is mandatory if you want to truly get from where you are to where you want to be. What are your most productive management times? Your most productive visionary times? Your most productive doctor times? Schedule your day, your month, and your year on paper or the computer and don't deviate. Block out your time on a daily, weekly, monthly, and annual basis for little-t time and big-T time.

Schedule your vacations—now. Not just before going away. Make sure you schedule them and adhere to them. That is time for you. No clinical work...maybe a vision or two over a beverage of your choice.

- Work in your practice when you are working in it.
- Work on your practice when you are working on it.
- And do work on you when you are not working on it or in it.

In Jack Canfield's Book, *The Success Principles*, he talks about two principles that I strongly believe in. They are:

1. **The Power Hour:** Essentially, dedicate one hour per day to meditation, working out, and reading something motivational, twenty minutes each. In a perfect world, you do this when you get up in the morning. Set your alarm an hour earlier and just do it.
    - 20 minutes of meditation
    - 20 minutes of reading
    - 20 minutes of exercise
2. **Scheduling Your Peak Times and Times Off Because Recreation Is time for Re-Creating:** I have personally found that my best thoughts and ideas come when I am about to go to sleep, driving, in the shower, or riding a bike. Now, don't get me wrong, driving and taking a shower are not recreation, but they do allow me for some creation time that I seem to miss otherwise.

As an entrepreneur, it is exquisitely hard to step away from your business baby. But if you can, that time of mental clarity very frequently will allow you to brainstorm and create. Whether it is on the beach, at the mountains, in the ocean, or just on the couch, recreation will frequently let you re-create your vision and subsequently reinvigorate your practice. Recreation is good physically, good spiritually, good mentally, and—believe it or not—good for business.

A quick heads-up: although long vacations seem to make sense, especially when you are trying to get away with your family, your business continues to exist in your absence. In a perfectly systematized world, you don't need to be there and the business will thrive in your absence. However, until you get to that level, a multitude of short, frequent getaways will be better for your mental wellbeing and the wellbeing of the business.

Schedule a bunch of five-day weekends or a four-day vacation and use the fifth day as Fireman's Day: in your house, put out the fires, clean up the messes and your desk, and return to work the next day without the proverbial guillotine over your neck. And when I say schedule them, I mean do it now. Put them on the books. In pen. Highlighted. Laminated. Unalterable. Make it happen so you can make it happen. By doing this you will have: something to look forward to avoid burn out and be refreshed every few weeks.

Tick-Tock, Tick-Tock

- 7 hours of sleep, minimum
- 10 hours of working in the business, includes commuting and actual work (note: 8 a.m. to 5 p.m. is really 7:30 a.m. to 5:30 p.m. when you add the commute)
- 2 hours of working on the business
- 2 hours for three meals, bathroom breaks, and personal hygiene
- 3 hours (180 minutes) for family, gym, leisure, reading

Those three hours are the most important minutes of your day, week, month, and life. Do not lose them, abuse them, and waste them. You can invest in your leisure time by reading, listening to books on your iPhone, and using the Internet for educational resources. Outsource those things you don't like to do (shopping, gardening). By the way, you can't pay somebody to do your pushups for you—it doesn't work that way.

Multi-Tasking

Some people think that multi-tasking is the solution to getting more time. However, if reports are correct, multi-tasking actually slows you down. No more than ninety minutes of focused time, followed by a fifteen-to-thirty-minute mental break is more effective and efficient than multi-tasking. In fact, if I remember this correctly, multi-tasking has a negative impact on each of the tasks, comparable to trying to work after smoking a joint.

If I Could Turn Back Time

Handling time is a challenge on all fronts—Big T and Little t.

There is no question that the sacrifices I personally made for the business were great for the business in the short haul. The clients, the patients, and the staff all benefited from my dedication and devotion to making the business thrive and grow.

For the first five years, there were no children to distract from doing it, doing it, doing it. So the focus on the little t at the expense of the big T most impacted my marriage. And then Brianna came along. And three years later Brooke came along. And now, the big T became a priority. Fortunately, the focus on the little t for the first five years and the resources from the E-Myth books had created a business that was ready to be sufficient without as much of my time.

There is no question that in life the ability to truly balance the personal and professional times will significantly impact your satisfaction as a technician, manager, and entrepreneur. And provide more personal time for your life.

If I could turn back time . . . If I knew then what I know now . . . There is no question that I would have spent much more time working on my business and much less time working in my business. And it is this concept of work that will be the center of Michael's next chapter.

CHAPTER

23

On the Subject of Work

Michael E. Gerber

As we learn we always change, and so our perception. This changed perception then becomes a new Teacher inside each of us.

—Hyemeyohsts Storm

In the business world, as the saying goes, the entrepreneur knows something about everything, the technician knows everything about something, and the telephone operator just knows everything.

In a veterinary practice, veterinarians see their natural work as the work of the technician. The Supreme Technician. Often to the exclusion of everything else.

After all, veterinarians get zero preparation working as a manager and spend no time thinking as an entrepreneur—those just aren't courses offered in today's veterinary schools. By the time they own their own veterinary practice, they're just doing it, doing it, doing it.

At the same time, they want everything—freedom, respect, money. Most of all, they want to rid themselves of meddling bosses and start their own practice. That way they can be their own boss and take home all the money. These veterinarians are in the throes of an entrepreneurial seizure.

Veterinarians who have been praised for their ability to handle difficult cases or their extensive knowledge of veterinary medicine believe they have what it takes to run a veterinary practice. It's not unlike the plumber who becomes a contractor because he's a great plumber. Sure, he may be a great plumber, but it doesn't necessarily follow that he knows how to build a practice that does this work.

It's the same for a veterinarian. So many of them are surprised to wake up one morning and discover that they're nowhere near as equipped for owning their own practice as they thought they were.

More than any other subject, work is the cause of obsessive-compulsive behavior by veterinarians.

Work. You've got to do it every single day.

Work. If you fall behind, you'll pay for it.

Work. There's either too much or not enough.

So many veterinarians describe work as what they do when they're busy. Some discriminate between the work they *could* be doing as veterinarians and the work they *should* be doing as veterinarians.

But according to the E-Myth, they're exactly the same thing. The work you *could* do and the work you *should* do as a veterinarian are identical. Let me explain.

Strategic Work vs. Tactical Work

Veterinarians can do only two kinds of work: strategic work and tactical work.

Tactical work is easier to understand, because it's what almost every veterinarian does almost every minute of every hour of every day. It's called getting the job done. It's called doing business.

Tactical work includes filing, billing, answering the telephone, handling media advertising services, researching new equipment, and seeing patients.

The E-Myth says that tactical work is all the work veterinarians find themselves doing in a veterinary practice to *avoid* doing the strategic work.

"I'm too busy," most veterinarians will tell you.

"How come nothing goes right unless I do it myself?" they complain in frustration.

Veterinarians say these things when they're up to their ears in tactical work. But most veterinarians don't understand that if they had done more strategic work, they would have less tactical work to do.

Please note that I said veterinarians ask these questions when they are doing strategic work. I didn't say these are the questions they necessarily answer.

That is the fundamental difference between strategic work and tactical work. Tactical work is all about *answers:* How to do this. How to do that.

Strategic work, in contrast, is all about *questions:* What practice are we really in? Why are we in that practice? Who specifically is our practice determined to serve? When will I sell this practice? How and where will this practice be doing business when I sell it? And so forth.

Not that strategic questions don't have answers. Veterinarians who commonly ask strategic questions know that once they ask such a question, they're already on their way to *envisioning* the answer. Question and answer are part of a whole. You can't find the right answer until you've asked the right question.

Tactical work is much easier, because the question is always more obvious. In fact, you don't ask the tactical question; instead, the question arises from a result you need to get or a problem you need to solve. Billing a patient is tactical work. Advising a patient is tactical work. Firing an employee is tactical work. Conducting an examination is tactical work.

Tactical work is the stuff you do every day in your practice. Strategic work is the stuff you plan to do to create an exceptional practice/business/enterprise.

In tactical work, the question comes from *out there* rather than *in here*. The tactical question is about something *outside* of you, whereas the strategic question is about something *inside* of you.

The tactical question is about something you *need* to do, whereas the strategic question is about something you *want* to do. Want versus need.

If tactical work consumes you,

- you are always reacting to something outside of you;
- your practice runs you; you don't run it;
- your employees run you; you don't run them,; and
- your life runs you, you don't run your life.

You must understand that the more strategic work you do, the more intentional your decisions, your practice, and your life become. *Intention* is the byword of strategic work.

Everything on the outside begins to serve you, to serve your vision, rather than forcing you to serve it. Everything you *need* to do is congruent with what you want to do. It means you have a vision, an aim, a purpose, a strategy, an *envisioned* result.

Strategic work is the work you do to *design* your practice, to design your life.

Tactical work is the work you do to *implement* the design created by strategic work.

Without strategic work, there is no design. Without strategic work, all that's left is keeping busy.

There's only one thing left to do. It's time to take action. But first, let's see what Peter has to say on the subject of work. ✤

CHAPTER

24

Hi Ho, Hi Ho, It's Off to Work I Go

Peter Weinstein, DVM, MBA

Early in the morning factory whistle blows.
Man rises from bed and puts on his clothes.
Man takes his lunch, walks out in the morning light.
It's the working, the working, just the working life.

—Bruce Springsteen, "Factory"

The major goal of this book is to change the way you think. To take and rearrange synapses from a focus on the day-to-day tactical work to a focus on the more global, strategic work. It's not easy. If it were easy, you wouldn't need this book.

Even as veterinarian wannabes, we were schooled in classes such as biology, chemistry, organic chemistry, biochemistry, physiology, anatomy, and physics that come with their own foundational principles that are so written in granite that they are immutable. In fact, for any healthcare profession, the educational process integrates very little, if any, independent thinking. So how would a practicing veterinarian even start to know how to reinitiate his or her imagination centers? It's not easy. But if you want to get out of the rut that you continue to deepen, you must.

Whenever I am at meetings with colleagues listening to their woes, I think back to my days as an associate, and then as a young business owner. The days when the appointment book controlled your life. When you had the skin talk, the puppy talk, the kitten talk, the vomiting talk, the diarrhea talk, and all of the repetitive conversations that you conducted going from room to room. The mundane became tedious. The tedious became routine. And the routine was what we did every day. It wasn't very motivating.

And then you went into surgery, which is best done the same way every time. The only real strategy was what to do if things went wrong. The same goes for handling anesthesia, dental cleanings, and radiographs. The vast majority of what we did on a daily basis was predictable.

When you progress from associate to owner, you might think that there is more wiggle room. There is if you find it, but for the most part, ownership is also a series of tactical tasks done repetitively without thought: pay bills, run payroll, order drugs, hire people, fire people. So, the technical skills that were developed to become a veterinarian are just translated to new tasks. And so it goes . . .

Hi Ho, Hi Ho, It's Off to Work You Go . . . Working in the Coal Mine

Essentially everything we do as clinicians is technical work and tactical work, with a designed outcome in mind—not a lot of independent thought processes allowed. This isn't a bad thing because it truly lends itself to the discussion of processes and systems that are the foundation for this tome.

When you think about it, veterinary medicine, for the most part, is a set of very predictable rituals. However, because you probably haven't thought about it that way, every time you do a task, you are re-creating the processes. Why not write down the processes and make them a system? Then all you have to do, as a manager or an entrepreneur, is work on the systems. Stop re-creating the wheel again and again and again.

Gotta Go to Work or *Get* to Go to Work

As a practitioner, the sixty-hour workweeks with satisfactory pay and unsatisfactory life style led to my need for a change. For three years or more, I worked my butt off in the exam room, in the surgery suite, in the treatment room, in the business office, at home, six (sometimes seven) days per week. We grew. I grew. We learned. I learned. But the work wore me down. The enthusiasm I had as a young owner eroded. The motivation to be there diminished. It was such a task just to get up in the morning and go to work. I was burning out and looking for an exit strategy. Was there a buyer out there? Anywhere?

The eventual epiphany that I had came when I decided I wanted to have greater control of my life and my ability to give back to my profession, to my kids, and to humankind. There is no way that I could be a Dilbert-like veterinarian, caught in my cubicle, simply doing it, doing it, doing it, and accomplish my personal purpose. I had to change the business to allow me to accomplish everything that the business could, thus allowing me to accomplish what I personally wanted to.

If you get up in the morning and *gotta* go to work, you have a job. There is no enthusiasm in the tasks you have to accomplish. Most of your staff feels this way. They, like you, are technicians doing tasks.

When you can change your work to a level of excitement that has you wanting to *get to go to work,* you have become a visionary strategist looking to see what is around the next corner.

As a tactician technician, you use your head, but mostly your hands to accomplish the busywork in a business. As a visionary, you use head, heart, and hands to do the work on the business—the strategy that gets your business closer to its primary aim and you closer to your life and your personal aim. This is what I did.

As a technician, I was paid a fee for the tasks I accomplished. Very limiting. Very finite. As an entrepreneur, the big-picture view created a business that gave more back in terms of value and meaning and results. And eventually it paid off because I was able to sell the business and work toward my personal primary aim, while concurrently leaving behind the legacy of a successful business entity that could thrive and survive.

Why? Why? Why?

This is a question I have asked myself, and I'm sure you have as well. Why did I become a veterinarian? Why did I decide to have my own business?

Did you become a veterinarian to become a dog-and-cat-repair person? Or to prevent racehorses from breaking down? Or to get more beef from a cow? Did you do that?

Did I open my own business to take care of pets' needs? Or my own needs? Was I able to do that?

Can you really be a successful veterinarian as defined by the tasks you do? And a successful veterinarian as defined by the achievements of your business?

The answer is *yes*. But you have to stop working *in* your business and start working *on* your business. The last chapter was about time, and you may still tell me you don't have time. And I'm going to tell you to *make* time! Schedule time. Let your staff know that you are not available for clients because you are working on the bigger picture. Schedule strategic time in the same way you schedule tactical time. You cannot create your vision when it is distracted or clouded by an itchy dog or a vomiting cat. Strategic time is business growth time from a long-term visionary standpoint, not from a quick-fix standpoint.

The Whine Train

As I speak with veterinarians these days, it becomes harder and harder to figure out what to do to be successful. Longer hours? More doctors? Closed Saturday? Fewer staff? Additional services? Fewer services? Too much month at the end of the money, too many out-of-money experiences, out-of-client experiences, and out-of-pocket experiences leading to out-of-body experiences and the perpetual Whine Train.

What is the Whine Train? *Why me?* Nobody seems to care as much as I do. People just don't show up for work and don't call. Where are all of the hard workers? Drug prices are too high. Clients aren't coming. Taxes go up. This is what happens when your focus is strictly the end of your nose. This is survival mode and not thriving mode.

Just stay on the same track, whining all the way.

Let Me Be Blunt

If you have ever watched the circus lineup of elephants, every elephant in the line has the same view. They each grab the tail of the elephant in front of them and follow along. Their view never changes and their vision is pretty limited. Of course, the elephant at the front is the one with the real vision—the open space ahead of him or her that will take them to places no elephant has seen before. Unless, of course, they grab the tail of the last elephant in line.

If you are not a lead elephant, your view is the same everyday and your vision is limited. You need to do the strategic work needed to become the lead elephant. The other elephants have only one task in mind: don't get pooped on. As the lead elephant, you set your vision and avoid getting pooped on.

This chapter on work is to get you motivated to be the lead elephant. Get a vision of your practice and your life as a final product. What does it look like? Don't get hung up on the details of the trip (that is so veterinarian of you); get excited about the outcome. And every day, work toward the destination. Use the ideas and tools outlined in the prior chapters and your long-lost imagination to create the business that will give you, your staff, your clients, and their pets the optimal experience. Learn to do what you love to do every day, get paid for it, and make sure that your business dream feeds your personal dreams as well.

Working in your business will give you a paycheck.

Working on your business will give you a life.

As you read this and ponder how the heck you are going to do it, realize that sitting there is great, but taking the first step is imperative. If you want to get from here to there, it won't happen on its own. It will take action, *your* action. Michael will motivate you to take the actions you need. So take the necessary action to turn the page. ✤

CHAPTER
25

On the Subject of Taking Action

Michael E. Gerber

Deliberation is the work of many men. Action, of one alone.
—Charles de Gaulle

It's time to get started, time to take action. Time to stop thinking about the old practice and start thinking about the new practice. It's not a matter of coming up with better practices; it's about reinventing the business of veterinary medicine.

And the veterinarian has to take personal responsibility for it.

That's you.

So sit up and pay attention!

You, the veterinarian, have to be interested. You cannot abdicate accountability for the business of veterinary medicine, the administration of veterinary medicine, or the finance of veterinary medicine.

Although the goal is to create systems into which veterinarians can plug reasonably competent people—systems that allow the practice to run without them—veterinarians must take responsibility for that happening.

I can hear the chorus now: "But we're veterinarians! We shouldn't have to know about this." To that I say: whatever. If you don't give a flip about your practice, fine—close your mind to new knowledge and accountability. But if you want to succeed, then you'd better step up and take responsibility, and you'd better do it now.

All too often, veterinarians take no responsibility for the business of a veterinary clinic, but instead delegate tasks without any understanding of what it takes to do them; without any interest in what their people are actually doing; without any sense of what it feels like to be at the front desk when a patient comes in and has to wait for forty-five minutes; and without any appreciation for the entity that is creating their livelihood.

Veterinarians can open the portals of change in an instant. All you have to do is say, "I don't want to do it that way anymore." Saying it will begin to set you free—even though you don't yet understand what the practice will look like after it's been reinvented.

This demands an intentional leap from the known into the unknown. It further demands that you live there—in the unknown—for a while. It means discarding the past, everything you once believed to be true.

Think of it as soaring rather than plunging.

Thought Control

You should now be clear about the need to organize your thoughts first, and then your business. Because the organization of your thoughts is the foundation for the organization of your business.

If we try to organize our business without organizing our thoughts, we will fail to attack the problem.

We have seen that organization is not simply time management. Nor is it people management. Nor is it tidying up desks or alphabetizing patient files. Organization is first, last, and always cleaning up the mess of our minds.

By learning how to *think* about a veterinary practice, by learning how to *think* about your priorities, and by learning how to *think* about your life, you'll prepare yourself to do righteous battle with the forces of failure.

Right thinking leads to right action—and now is the time to take action. Because it is only through action that you can translate thoughts into movement in the real world, and, in the process, find fulfillment.

So, first *think* about what you want to do. Then *do* it. Only in this way will you be fulfilled.

How do you put the principles we've discussed in this book to work in your veterinary practice? To find out, follow me down the path once more:

1. *Create a story about your practice.* Your story should be an idealized version of your veterinary practice, a vision of what the preeminent veterinarian in your field should be and why. Your story must become the very heart of your practice. It must become the spirit that mobilizes it, as well as everyone who walks through the doors. Without this story, your practice will be reduced to plain work.

2. *Organize your practice so that it breathes life into your story.* Unless your practice can faithfully replicate your story in action, it all becomes fiction. In that case, you'd be better off not telling your story at all. And without a story, you'd be better off leaving your practice the way it is and just hoping for the best.

Here are some tips for organizing your veterinary practice:

- Identify the key functions of your practice.
- Identify the essential processes that link those functions.
- Identify the results you have determined your practice will produce.
- Clearly state in writing how each phase will work.

Take it step by step. Think of your practice as a program, a piece of software, a system. It is a collaboration, a collection of processes dynamically interacting with one another.

Of course, your practice is also people.

3. *Engage your people in the process.* Why is this the third step rather than the first? Because, contrary to the advice most business experts will give you, you must never engage your people in the process until you yourself are clear about what you intend to do.

The need for consensus is a disease of today's addled mind. It's a product of our troubled and confused times. When people don't know what to believe in, they often ask others to tell them. To ask is not to lead but to follow.

The prerequisite of sound leadership is first to know where you wish to go.

And so, "What do I want?" becomes the first question; not, "What do they want?" In your own practice, the vision must first be yours. To follow another's vision is to abdicate your personal accountability, your leadership role, your true power.

In short, the role of leader cannot be delegated or shared. And without leadership, no veterinary practice will ever succeed.

Despite what you have been told, win-win is a secondary step, not a primary one. The opposite of win-win is not necessarily they lose.

Let's say "they" can win by choosing a good horse. The best choice will not be made by consensus. "Guys, what horse do you think we should ride?" will always lead to endless and worthless discussions. By the time you're done jawing, the horse will have already left the post.

Before you talk to your people about what you intend to do in your practice and why you intend to do it, you need to reach agreement with yourself.

It's important to know (1) exactly what you want, (2) how you intend to proceed, (3) what's important to you and what isn't, and (4) what you want the practice to be and how you want it to get there.

Once you have that agreement, it's critical that you engage your people in a discussion about what you intend to do and why. Be clear—both with yourself and with them.

The Story

The story is paramount because it is your vision. Tell it with passion and conviction. Tell it with precision. Never hurry a great story. Unveil it slowly. Don't mumble or show embarrassment. Never apologize or display false modesty. Look your audience in the eyes and tell your story as though it is the most important one they'll ever hear about business. Your business. The business into which you intend to pour your heart, your soul, your intelligence, your imagination, your time, your money, and your sweaty persistence.

Get into the storytelling zone. Behave as though it means everything to you. Show no equivocation when telling your story.

These tips are important because you're going to tell your story over and over—to patients, to new and old employees, to veterinarians, to staff members, and to your family and friends. You're going to tell it at your church or synagogue, to your card-playing or fishing buddies, and to organizations such as Kiwanis, Rotary, YMCA, Hadassah, and Boy Scouts.

There are few moments in your life when telling a great story about a great business is inappropriate.

If it is to be persuasive, you must love your story. Do you think Walt Disney loved his Disneyland story? Or Ray Kroc his McDonald's story? What about Fred Smith at Federal Express? Or Debbie Fields at Mrs. Fields Cookies? Or Tom Watson Jr. at IBM?

Do you think these people loved their stories? Do you think others loved (and still love) to hear them? I daresay all successful entrepreneurs have loved the story of their business. Because that's what true entrepreneurs do. They tell stories that come to life in the form of their business.

Remember: A great story never fails. A great story is always a joy to hear.

In summary, you first need to clarify, both for yourself and for your people, the story of your practice. Then you need to detail the process your practice must go through to make your story become reality.

I call this the business development process. Others call it reengineering, continuous improvement, reinventing your practice, or total quality management.

Whatever you call it, you must take three distinct steps to succeed:

- *Innovation*. Continue to find better ways of doing what you do.
- *Quantification*. Once that is achieved, quantify the impact of these improvements on your practice.
- *Orchestration*. Once these improvements are verified, orchestrate this better way of running your practice so that it becomes your standard, to be repeated time and again.

In this way, the system works—no matter who's using it. And you've built a practice that works consistently, predictably, systematically. A practice you can depend on to operate exactly as promised, every single time.

Your vision, your people, your process—all linked.

A superior veterinary practice is a creation of your imagination, a product of your mind. So fire it up and get started! Now let's check in and see what Peter has to say about taking action. ✤

CHAPTER

26

First Act or Last Act—Your Choice

Peter Weinstein, DVM, MBA

Well, I'm not gonna leave you alone. I want you to get mad! I don't want you to protest. I don't want you to riot. I don't want you to write to your congressman because I wouldn't know what to tell you to write. I don't know what to do about the depression and the inflation and the Russians and the crime in the street. All I know is that first you've got to get mad. You've got to say, 'I'm a human being, Goddamnit! My life has value!' So I want you to get up now. I want all of you to get up out of your chairs. I want you to get up right now and go to the window. Open it, and stick your head out, and yell, 'I'm mad as hell, and I'm not going to take this anymore!'

—Howard Beale, *Network*

Yogi says, "When you come to a fork in the road, take it." So here you are. Over the many pages, we have shared many thoughts on the classic veterinary practice as a small business, a business where many of you are held hostage from life and family and enjoyment. Your practice should have been created to free you to do what you want to do. Instead you are a technician who had an entrepreneurial seizure working for a lunatic just doing it, doing it, doing it. And you are afraid about what to do next. Nobody can make that decision for you. You are free to take action. In fact, you must. You need to make it so. Nobody else can or will.

You have reached the end of a journey—at least the journey through this book. In many cases after you get done reading a book, you put it on a bookshelf or delete it from your iPad and go find the next book to read. Is that what you plan to do with this book?

This book is a call to action. It is not a novel about life; it is a fact-filled discussion on how to make your life *better*. If you treat it like a novel and read it and move on, you have totally missed the point. On the other hand, if you look at it as a guide to taking that first step toward success, you have it figured out.

Where else are you going to see a section started with Yogi Berra and ended with Sir Isaac Newton? Newton's first law...you don't remember it? See if this looks familiar:

"*A body at rest tends to stay rest; a body in motion will stay in motion.*"

So what do you plan to do? Act and succeed or snooze and lose?

Déjà Vu

My Story: In the spring of 1989, I opened a small animal hospital in the burgeoning city of Laguna Hills, California. It was there that I intended to provide veterinary services with a Mayo Clinic–level of care in a client-service environment found only at Nordstrom's. This practice was to provide a friendly, comfortable, and knowledgeable refuge for our clients to receive medical, surgical, dental, and well-care from a veterinary standpoint, and boarding and grooming from an ancillary service standpoint. It would provide a comfortable work environment where staff members could find careers, and associate veterinarians could find the practice of their dreams. It would provide an example of how to deliver veterinary services in the Twentieth

Century as a model for my colleagues. And its community involvement would support pets and pet owners in need. All of this would provide for me a sufficient income and quality of life to allow me to globally make a difference in the veterinary world, and the world in general.

That was my dream. I knew it. I believed in it. But I really didn't share it. It was tattooed inside of my eyelids and heart. At first, I wasn't comfortable sharing it with anybody. It was so far-fetched. In fact, what you are reading hasn't been shared globally with anybody until right now. This was my primary aim before I knew it was my primary aim. And it got lost in just doing it, doing it, doing it.

In writing this book, I have relived the many days, weeks, months, and years of pain that I went through trying to find the way out of the daily doldrums. I have to thank Michael Gerber and his E-Myth for the permission to escape the box. This book is my giving back to him and to you. At the same time, I am giving you the permission that I was looking for: *take action!*

Taking the First Step

Ancient Chinese Philosopher, Lao Tzu, may have said it best: "Do the difficult things while they are easy, and do the great things while they are small. A journey of a thousand miles must begin with a single step."

I have two daughters, and watching them learn to walk taught me so many lessons:

- Perseverance
- Trial and error
- Taking risks

Watching a baby learn to walk, you see them first pull themselves up, steady themselves, and then shuffle forward. And then they fall. They pick themselves up and try again. They fall. And repeat. If babies didn't take that first step, if they didn't try, we would all be sitting in diapers waiting for the world to come to us. Your practice is very much like a baby. If you don't take the first step, you aren't going anywhere—remember Newton's First law.

The veterinary field notoriously fears change, action, growth, new things, the unknown, and being different. It is a body at rest.

However, you as a veterinarian have a strong history of taking action and showing determination. From elementary school, through high school and college, and finally getting into veterinary school, you suffered, sacrificed, went against the grain, and you succeeded. Up until now, you didn't fear action or determination. Why now?

We are not talking about change for the sake of change, nor action for the sake of action. We are talking about strategically determined action that supports you and your practice's objectives and aims. The changes are tactical strikes to get you closer to your vision.

How do you take the first step? You need a primary aim and objectives, the targets for which you are aiming. Like the baby learning to walk to be able to reach new things, you need to have a reason to change. What is your vision? What do you want your story to be? You read mine. Create yours. Now go get it!

Ready-Fire-Aim

You have created your target—so go for it! But I can't. I know I should, but I can't. Well, stop should-ing all over yourself and take the first step. I can see you now:

You are ready.

You aim and then you stop.

So, you aim again.

And you stop…

Performance anxiety.

Fear.

Analysis paralysis.

Try *ready-fire-aim*. Try something; if it doesn't work, recalibrate and try again. That's called feedback and it's a good thing. It helps you straighten your aim and get you closer to your target. With feedback, the faster you fail, the faster you learn.

Try *act-review-recalibrate-repeat*. You will find that after you fall and get up, falling is easier! And more questions will arise that will help. Questions are a key to action. Asking question like:

- What would happen if?
- What would happen if not?
- What's the best that could happen?
- What's the worst that could happen?
- Are there other options that are better?

This is a great time to ask questions, discuss, think, analyze, and do your due diligence. Ask strategic questions. These questions will lead to tactical answers and tactical action—but be careful of analysis paralysis. Then take that first step.

Swoosh

That's the Nike symbol. And one of Nike's slogans is: *Just Do It!* Your business needs to support you personal life dreams. If it isn't doing so and you are simply an employee of the business you own and not reaping the awards of ownership and entrepreneurship, talk less and act more. Talking does not equal doing. Stop thinking about doing it and *just do it*. Planning does not equal action.

I am not sure where I heard this quote, but it is a mantra for small business change agents: *More businesses fail from failing to take action rather than from taking the wrong action*.

It is so true. It is time to convert all of these pages of information into the knowledge needed to put the pedal to the metal and get moving. Stop crawling and pull yourself up and take that first step.

And I bet you didn't think of this: with your newfound understanding of systems, you can create an action system or decision-making system that will take you step by step from thinking to discussing to choosing to acting. All within twenty-four hours.

What Got You Here Won't Get You There

Sure, there were times I was scared about opening my practice.

Sure, there were times I was scared about moving my practice.

Sure, there were times I was scared about expanding my practice.

Sure, there were times I was scared about selling my practice.

But you know what? I was more scared about doing nothing, and the decision to do *something* was less scary. We know you are scared or you would have done something already. So just know that we are here to be your cheerleaders. Ever hear this one?

A-C-T-I-O-N

Action, action

We want action!

Create a business that supports your life dream and your personal life dreams. Create a business that tells your story, a story that others will tell long after you have left the business.

"So many of our dreams at first seem impossible, then they seem improbable, and then when we summon the will, they soon become inevitable," says Christopher Reeve who portrayed Superman in the movies. What is your dream? What is your first step?

We look forward to hearing your story and being there to share in your happiness and success. ✤

AFTERWORD

Michael E. Gerber

For more than three decades, I've applied the E-Myth principles I've shared with you here to the successful development of thousands of small businesses throughout the world. Many have been veterinary practices—from small companies to large corporations, with veterinarians specializing in markets all over the country.

Few rewards are greater than seeing these E-Myth principles improve the work and lives of so many people. Those rewards include seeing these changes:

- Lack of clarity—clarified.
- Lack of organization—organized.
- Lack of direction—shaped into a path that is clearly, lovingly, passionately pursued.
- Lack of money or money poorly managed—money understood instead of coveted; created instead of chased; wisely spent or invested instead of squandered.
- Lack of committed people—transformed into a cohesive community working in harmony toward a common goal; discovering one another and themselves in the process; all the while expanding their understanding, their know-how, their interest, their attention.

After working with so many veterinarians, I know that a practice can be much more than what most become. I also know that nothing is preventing you from making your practice all that it can be. It takes only desire and the perseverance to see it through.

In this book—the next of its kind in the E-Myth Expert series—the E-Myth principles have been complemented and enriched by stories from real-life veterinarians, such as Peter, who has put these principles to use in his practice. Peter had the desire and perseverance to achieve success beyond his wildest dreams. Now you, too, can join them their ranks.

I hope this book has helped you clear your vision and set your sights on a very bright future.

To your practice and your life, good growing.

ABOUT THE AUTHOR

Michael E. Gerber

Michael E. Gerber is the international legend, author, and thought leader behind the E-Myth series of books, including *The E-Myth Revisited, E-Myth Mastery, The E-Myth Manager, The E-Myth Enterprise, The Most Successful Small Business in the World and Awakening the Entrepreneur Within.* Collectively, Mr. Gerber's books have sold millions of copies worldwide. Michael Gerber is the founder of Michael E. Gerber Companies, E-Myth Worldwide, The Dreaming Room™, and his newest venture, Design, Build, Launch & Grow™. Since 1977, Mr. Gerber's companies have served the business development needs of over 70,000 business clients in over 145 countries. Regarded by his avid followers as the thought leader of entrepreneurship worldwide, Mr. Gerber has been called by Inc. Magazine, "the world's #1 small business guru." A highly sought-after speaker and strategist, who has single handedly been accountable for the transformation of small business worldwide, Michael lives with his wife, Luz Delia, in Carlsbad, California.

ABOUT THE CO-AUTHOR

Peter Weinstein, DVM, MBA

Dr. Peter Weinstein wanted to be a veterinarian from the age of twelve. He fulfilled his dream by attending Cornell University (BS) and the University of Illinois (DVM). He is the classic E-Myth entrepreneur. As a young associate he had the entrepreneurial seizure, started his own practice, and suffered through doing it, doing it, doing it. While running his practice six days a week, he went back to school to work on his MBA at night. Concurrently, he discovered The E-Myth and Michael Gerber. With an understanding of systems and business, he was able grow his practice, move it, and eventually sell it to a corporate consolidator. Through his company, PAW Consulting, and other ventures, he has worked with practices all over the world, and speaks and writes about practice success. Additionally, he has been an advocate for the veterinary profession in Southern California, California, and the United States. While doing all of this, he maintains his current role as Executive Director of the Southern California Veterinary Medical Association. Peter lives with his wife, Sharon, two daughters, Brianna and Brooke, two dogs, and a bird in Tustin, California.

ABOUT THE SERIES

The E-Myth Expert series brings Michael E. Gerber's proven E-Myth philosophy to a wide variety of different professional business areas. The E-Myth, short for "Entrepreneurial Myth," is simple: Too many small businesses fail to grow because their leaders think like technicians, not entrepreneurs. Gerber's approach gives small enterprise leaders practical, proven methods that have already helped transform tens of thousands of businesses. Let the E-Myth Expert series boost your professional business today!

Books in the series include:

The E-Myth Attorney
The E-Myth Accountant
The E-Myth Optometrist
The E-Myth Chiropractor
The E-Myth Financial Advisor
The E-Myth Landscape Contractor
The E-Myth Architect
The E-Myth Real Estate Brokerage
The E-Myth Insurance Store
The E-Myth Dentist
The E-Myth Nutritionist
The E-Myth Bookkeeper
The E-Myth Veterinarian

Forthcoming books in the series include:
The E-Myth Real Estate Investor
. . . and 300 more industries and professions

Learn more at: www.michaelegerber.com/co-author

Have you created an E-Myth enterprise? Would you like to become a co-author of an E-Myth book in your industry? Go to www.michaelegerber.com/co-author.

THE MICHAEL E. GERBER ENTREPRENEUR'S LIBRARY

It Keeps Growing . . .

Thank you for reading another E-Myth Vertical book.

Who do you know who is an expert in their industry?

Who has applied the E-Myth to the improvement of their practice as Peter Weinsten has?

Who can add immense value to others in his or her industry by sharing what he or she has learned?

Please share this book with that individual and share that individual with us.

✤

We at Michael E. Gerber Companies are determined to transform the state of small business and entrepreneurship worldwide. *You can help.*

To find out more, email us at Michael E. Gerber Partners, at gerber@michaelegerber.com.

To find out how *YOU* can apply the E-Myth to *YOUR* practice, contact us at gerber@michaelegerber.com.

Thank you for living your Dream, and changing the world.

MICHAEL E. GERBER PARTNERS
Authors of Business Design

Michael E. Gerber, Co-Founder/Chairman
Michael E. Gerber Companies™
Creator of The E-Myth Evolution™
P.O. Box 131195, Carlsbad, CA 92013
760-752-1812 O • 760-752-9926 F
gerber@michaelegerber.com
www.michaelegerber.com

Join The Evolution℠

Attend the Dreaming Room™ Trainings
www.michaelegerber.com/dreaming-room

Awaken the Entrepreneur Within You
www.michaelegerber.com/facilitator-training

Michael E. Gerber Partners
www.michaelegerber.com/are-you-the-one

Listen to the Michael E. Gerber Radio Show
www.blogtalkradio.com/michaelegerber

Watch the latest videos
www.youtube.com/michaelegerber

Connect on LinkedIn
www.linkedin.com/in/michaelegerber

Connect on Facebook
www.facebook.com/MichaelEGerberCo

Follow on Twitter
http://twitter.com/michaelegerber

CPSIA information can be obtained
at www.ICGtesting.com
Printed in the USA
LVOW12*0142231016
508891LV00001BA/1/P

9 781618 350336